RESEARCH AND INFORMATION
GUIDES IN BUSINESS, INDUSTRY,
AND ECONOMIC INSTITUTIONS

T0303972

NASDAQ

RESEARCH AND INFORMATION GUIDES IN BUSINESS, INDUSTRY AND ECONOMIC INSTITUTIONS

WAHIB NASRALLAH
General Editor

NASDAQ

A Guide to Information Sources

Lucy Heckman

Routledge
New York and London / 2001

Published in 2001 by
Routledge
2 Park Square, Milton Park, Abingdon, Oxfordshire OX14 4RN
711 Third Avenue, New York, NY 10017
First issued in paperback 2014
Routledge is an imprint of the Taylor and Francis Group, an informa business

Library of Congress Cataloging-in-Publication Data
Heckman, Lucy
    NASDAQ : a guide to information sources / Lucy Heckman.
    ISBN 978-0-8153-2118-7 (hbk)
    ISBN 978-0-415-76377-6 (pbk)
Cataloging-in-Publication Data for this title is available from the
    Library of Congress

CONTENTS

ACKNOWLEDGMENTS

I would like to thank Dr. James Benson, Dean of St. John's University Libraries for his generous support. Thanks are also due to my colleagues on the faculty, staff, and administation of St. John's University. Thanks to all those in the Interlibrary Loan Department for their help in tracking down and ordering items for me.

Thanks are also due to:

Nasdaq MarketSite
Queens Borough Public Library
St. John's University Law Library
New York Public Library. Science, Industry, and Business Library
Hofstra University

Special thanks are due to individuals who responded to my various inquiries and who have generously either sent me citations or copies of their work. They include William Christie of Vanderbilt University, Allen Kleidon of Cornerstone Research, David Casserly of NASD, and Dean Furbush of Economists, Inc. Thanks also to those at NASD/Nasdaq who answered my various questions and were most helpful.

INTRODUCTION

As I write this introduction, the Nasdaq Stock Market is looking forward to its Thirtieth Anniversary on February 8, 2001. Although Nasdaq is a relative newcomer on the securities industry scene, it has made quite an impact. It has weathered the storm of a major stock market crash in October 1987 and investigations by the Securities and Exchange Commission and the U.S. Justice Department in 1994-1996. It has grown and expanded to an active and internationally focused exchange.

The Nasdaq Stock Market: A Guide to Information Sources gathers together selected materials including books, dissertations, scholarly articles, working papers, empirical studies, newspaper and magazine articles, special studies, and government documents. The Internet is a repository of a large selection of information sources which include the National Association of Securities Dealers (NASD)/Nasdaq "family" of web sites and full-text journal and newspaper articles found in online databases.

This book consists of English language primary and secondary sources on Nasdaq. Dates of materials covered range from Nasdaq's roots in the founding of its parent company NASD, which was established as a result of the Maloney Act in 1938 through June 2000. Materials selected were located through scanning of periodical and newspaper indexes, both print and nonprint; online full-text databases, including ABI/INFORM, JSTOR, and ScienceDirect; Nasdaq/NASD web sites; and related web sites including Economists, Inc. Copies of materials were examined at local public and academic libraries. Those materials not available in the area were obtained through the St. John's

University Interlibrary Loan Department or by direct request to the authors.

Each annotated item has been assigned an entry number and items are indexed according to those numbers by author, title, and subject. Since some sources fall into several categories, cross-references are provided. Appendixes containing lists of indexes and abstracts, serial publications, online databases, and web sites are arranged alphabetically.

It should be noted here that Nasdaq is also referred to as NASDAQ by authors and editors, especially in materials of the 1970s and 1980s. In 1990, NASDAQ became known as the Nasdaq Stock Market.

The Nasdaq Stock Market: A Guide to Information Sources is not designed to provide a detailed history. It is hoped that a monograph or book, detailing Nasdaq's first thirty years will be written. Chapter I is an overview of the history of Nasdaq and its background with the founding of NASD. Also included in the Appendixes are names of Nasdaq/NASD presidents and a Chronology of the Nasdaq's history. A brief overview of historical events and key documents for specific time periods have been included with each time period covered in chapters. This guide is designed to serve as a starting point for locating sources and for research about Nasdaq.

NASDAQ

A Guide to
Information Sources

CHAPTER I
ORGANIZATION AND HISTORY

I. Organization

The Nasdaq Stock Market began on February 8, 1971 as a subsidiary company of the National Association of Securities Dealers, Inc. or NASD. The NASD, in existence since 1939, is also the parent company of NASD Regulation, Inc., an independent subsidiary charged with regulating the securities industry and the Nasdaq.

The mission statement of Nasdaq is as follows: "To facilitate capital formation in the public and private sector by developing, operating and regulating the most liquid, efficient, and fair securities market for the ultimate benefit and protection of the investor." (source: Nasdaq web site: http://http://www.nasdaq.com/about.mission.stm)

The members of the NASD Board of Governors are divided between non-member public representatives and industry staff members. Each Board member is elected to serve a term of office. The NASD Regulation and Nasdaq Board members are also part of the full NASD Board. The American Stock Exchange, also a subsidiary, has its own eighteen member Board. Additionally, all boards have separate committees and advisory boards. NASD is responsible for regulating the securities industry, Nasdaq, and the Amex. Leadership of the NASD is by its Chairman and Chief Executive Officer.

Nasdaq's main operating divisions are: Trade and Market Services, which is responsible for interface with market making, brokerage, and data vendor communities and develop systems including SelectNet and SOES; Issuer Services is responsible for retaining and adding new listings on Nasdaq; Investor Services is in charge of advertising and marketing for Nasdaq and has developed Nasdaq's web site; Market Operations, in Trumbull, Connecticut, keeps the market systems operating; Technology Services is responsible for the development and maintenance of telecommunications and computer network for quote dissemination, order routing, and trade reporting; and Nasdaq International Ltd., located in London, England, aims to help overseas expansion so foreign markets can have access to Nasdaq listings.

At present, approximately 5100 companies representing various industries and including companies ranging from small and growing to large corporations in both the United States and in other countries. Among industries represented are: banking, biotechnology, computer, finance, industrials, insurance, telecommunications, and transportation. Among notable companies listed on Nasdaq are Microsoft Corporation, Dell Computer Corporation, Intel Corporation, and MCI WORLDCOM, Inc.

Nasdaq is the world's first electronic-based stock market and operates under a system where market makers compete with one another for best buying and selling prices. Market makers are comprised of approximately 479 broker/dealer firms. Market makers use their own capital to buy and sell Nasdaq securities. ECNs or Electronic Communications Networks operate as market participants within the Nasdaq network. ECNs display one or two sided quotes, reflecting actual orders, and allow market makers and institutions an anonymous way of entering orders in to the marketplace. ECNs must be approved by the SEC as an alternative trading system (ATS).

The Nasdaq Stock Market is comprised of two separate markets: the Nasdaq National Market and the Nasdaq SmallCap Market. The Nasdaq National Market companies, include large corporations that must meet demanding financial and corporate governance standards to be listed. Currently, approximately 3800 securities are listed on the Nasdaq National Market. The Nasdaq SmallCap Market, comprised of 1000 companies, must meet the same corporate governance standards as the National Market, but financial criteria is not as strict.

Nasdaq's corporate governance standards relate to such factors as the distribution of annual reports; a minimum of two independent directors; an audit committee, the majority of which are independent directors; an annual shareholder meeting; quorum requirement; solicitation of proxies; shareholder approval for certain corporate actions; and voting rights.

To maintain a fair and orderly market, regulation is maintained by Nasdaq's MarketWatch Department and by Market Regulation, a division of NASD Regulation. Market Regulation operates within three units: Quality of Markets, Compliance and Surveillance, and Market Making Examination/Market Integrity. If any violations are found, Market Regulation will prosecute the matter and ensure imposition of appropriate sanctions. Nasdaq's MarketWatch Department, created in 1996, performs real-time online surveillance and is divided into two areas: StockWatch and TradeWatch. StockWatch monitors price and volume activity and reviews press releases from Nasdaq companies, providing an alert to events that could trigger a possible trading halt. TradeWatch conducts real-time monitoring of trading activity in the Nasdaq Stock Market.

Nasdaq Indices are: the Nasdaq Composite, Industry Specific Indices, Nasdaq-100 Index, Nasdaq Financial-100 Index, Nasdaq Financial-100 Index, Nasdaq National Market Composite Index. The Nasdaq Composite measures market value of all domestic and foreign common stocks listed on Nasdaq. Industry-specific indices measures eight industry specific sub-indices for Bank, Biotechnology, Computer, Finance, Industrial, Insurance, Telecommunications, and Transportation. The Nasdaq-100 Index includes the largest non-financial companies listed on Nasdaq; companies listed are required to have a minimum average daily trading volume of 100,000 shares. The Nasdaq Financial-100 Index is comprised of 100 of the largest financial organizations listed on Nasdaq. The Nasdaq National Market Composite Index consists of companies included in the Nasdaq Composite Index that are listed on the Nasdaq National Market.

Nasdaq's primary computing system is located in Trumbull, Connecticut and its backup system is located in Rockville, Maryland. Under the current system, 2500 Nasdaq transactions per second are possible and as many as three billion shares a day.

II. History

The beginnings of Nasdaq may be traced to the founding of its parent, the National Association of Securities Dealers, Inc. in August 1939. The NASD was established under the Maloney Act, an amendment (section 15A) to the Securities Exchange Act of 1934. The Maloney Act was sponsored by Senator Francis T. Maloney of

Connecticut and adopted in 1938. The first draft of the Maloney Act was dated November 4, 1937. A series of conferences followed relating to content, form, and concept of the draft. On January 18, 1938, the Maloney Act was formally introduced in the United States Senate and subsequently, became law on June 25, 1938. A drafting committee was appointed by the Governing Committee of the Investment Bankers Conference, Inc. to draw up a certificate of incorporation, bylaws, rules of fair practice, and a code of procedure for handling trade practice complaints. The drafting committee worked closely with the Securities and Exchange Commission to prepare this document. On March 18, 1939, the Investment Bankers Conference and the SEC submitted proposals for registration of the Investment Bankers Conference as a registered national securities association. The initial registration statement of the NASD, as successor to the Investment Bankers Conference, was filed with the SEC on July 20, 1939 and was approved by the SEC on August 7, 1939.

In 1939 NASD had 1500 broker-dealer members; this number expanded to 4771 members in 1961. The NASD bylaws, in accordance with the Maloney Act, shall be open to all brokers and dealers authorized to transact any branch of the investment banking and securities business in the United States.

In 1961, Congress authorized the Securities and Exchange Committee to conduct a special study of the securities markets. The resultant printed report was issued in 1963. Among the Special Study's recommendations was to prepare an automated over-the-counter market. The National Association of Securities Dealers (NASD) was charged with the planning and implementation of this automated market. In 1966, a special Automation Committee was formed by NASD; this Committee investigated the possibility of automated quotations in the OTC market. The Automation Committee selected the Bunker-Ramo Corporation of Trumbull, Connecticut to built and operate an automated system, under the direction of NASD. Subsequently, NASD signed a seven-year contract with Bunker Ramo in December 1968.

By 1968, the basic structure of the National Association of Securities Dealers Automated Quotation System (NASDAQ) was set and organized into: Level I which would provide representative bid and ask quotations for Nasdaq issues; Level II for the information of financial institutions and trading departments and would display quotations of all market makers in all Nasdaq securities, and Level III service which would allow market makers to change/update their quotes. Actual construction of Nasdaq commenced in 1968. The Bunker-Ramo Corporation owned the Nasdaq system when NASD exercised its five-year option and purchased the automated system in 1976 for $10 million. Subsequently, the Harris Terminal was introduced in 1980, succeeding the Bunker-Ramo terminal. A central computer facility was established at Trumbull, Connecticut, and on February 8, 1971 Nasdaq began operation.

Nasdaq continued to grow and expand, and in July 1980, Nasdaq provided highest bid and lowest ask from all market makers in a security, replacing the representative, median quotations. At the time, higher qualification standards were required by companies who wished to list securities on Nasdaq. In April 1982, the Nasdaq National Market was started with 40 of the most active Nasdaq securities. At the end of 1982, share volume in 84 Nasdaq National Market Securities exceeded the volume in all 950 Amex securities. In 1984, the Small Order Execution System or SOES was introduced and designated to automatically execute small orders against the best quotations. In 1986, Nasdaq opened an Operations Center in Rockville, Maryland; this Center provides full back up to the computer system in Trumbull, Connecticut. The Nasdaq Workstation was introduced in 1987, providing more efficient trade and volume reporting, quote updating, and real-time monitoring of Nasdaq issues.

The October 1987 Stock Market Crash led to several changes for Nasdaq. The Brady Commission reported that during the week of October 19, 1987, some Nasdaq market makers formally withdrew from market making and did not answer phones. To prevent this from happening again, NASD strictly limited the acceptable reasons for Nasdaq market makers to withdraw from market making. Additionally, the Nasdaq Workstation, which enhances speed and efficiency, was provided to market makers. Other changes in Nasdaq brought about as a result of the Crash were: mandatory participation in SOES for all market makers in Nasdaq National Market securities; introduction of the Order Confirmation Transaction System, permitting automated execution for trades up to 100,000 shares; institution of trading halts when companies receive material news; and expansion of disclosure to investors regarding qualifications and disciplinary histories of registered representatives and member firms. In 1988, Nasdaq initiated the Advanced Computerized Execution System (ACES), an order-routing and execution system. In 1989, Nasdaq launched the Automated Confirmation Transaction (ACT), featuring a same-day trade comparison capability.

In 1990, the Nasdaq formally changed its name to the Nasdaq Stock Market. SelectNet was begun in 1990, and provided an online screen negotiation and execution service. In November 1990, the Order Confirmation Service (OTC)'s name was given added features, including the ability to send broadcast orders to all market makers in a specific stock and renamed SelectNet.

The year 1994 was a major one for Nasdaq with two landmark events. First of all, the Nasdaq Stock Market surpassed the New York Stock Exchange in annual share volume. Second, results of an academic study of the Nasdaq were released to the public, triggering major investigations, lawsuits, and, ultimately, changes to NASD and Nasdaq. William Christie and Paul Schultz, professors at Vanderbilt University and Ohio State University, respectively, prepared an academic paper. Their findings were released in May 1994 to several news services. These findings were to appear in an article, "Why do Nasdaq Market Makers Avoid Odd-Eighth Quotes" in the *Journal of Finance*. Their academic study reported findings of their study of market statistics, asked why Nasdaq market makers avoid odd-eighth quotes and included implications of collusion among market makers. Reaction to this study was instantaneous: law suits were filed by investors and the SEC and U.S. Department of Justice became involved in investigations of the NASD and Nasdaq. The NASD commissioned Senator Warren Rudman to prepare an investigative report and recommendations for Nasdaq/NASD. The Rudman Report was released in Fall 1995.

Reports were published by the Department of Justice, the SEC, and the Rudman Commission. The Department of Justice reported that the market makers were in violation of Section 1 of the Sherman Antitrust Act and the market makers were told to abandon the practice of avoiding odd-eighth quotes. Additionally, market makers were prohibited from harassing other market makers. The SEC reported that not using odd-eighth quotes was antitcompetitive and the NASD was blamed for not overseeing Nasdaq and ignoring the anti-competitive practices. The Rudman Report made recommendations including establishment of the NASD Regulation, Inc. or NASDR, the regulatory unit of NASD, effectively separating regulatory responsibilities from ownership and operation of Nasdaq. The Nasdaq MarketWatch Department was established in 1996 after recommendation by Rudman Committee.

During 1996-97, the decimalization system was considered by the

U.S. securities markets, including Nasdaq. This is currently being considered by Nasdaq for 2001 implementation. In 1997, the SEC approved Nasdaq's request to start quoting in 1/16ths. In 1998, a merger between the NASD and Amex creates the Nasdaq-Amex Market Group. The Nasdaq Stock Exchange is a part of this group. Two separate web sites are available for Nasdaq and Amex and separate statistics are included in annual reports and Fact Books. The year 1998 also marked the beginning of the Nasdaq United Kingdom web site which was created to give investors in the UK information on U.S. and European stocks. In December 1997, a large class-action, private lawsuit against several major market makers was settled for a reported $1 billion in damages. In 1998, a merger took place between the NASD and the American Stock Exchange, forming the Nasdaq-Amex Market Group.

In 1999, Nasdaq achieved status as the largest U.S. stock market by dollar volume and, at several times throughout the year, breaks share and dollar volume records. The year 2000 marked growing expansion and investigation of future quoting in decimals.

The Nasdaq will celebrate its thirtieth anniversary on February 8, 2001. Nasdaq's first thirty years were those of great growth and innovation and it is now looking toward further global expansion and technological advances.

For further information about organization and history consult Appendix I for the Nasdaq Chronology and Appendix II for a list of officers of NASD and Nasdaq.

CHAPTER II
DICTIONARIES, ENCYCLOPEDIAS,
GENERAL GUIDES, HISTORIES

The following materials were selected to provide reference information and background reading regarding Nasdaq. Included are encyclopedias and dictionaries and the helpful source, *Nasdaq Backgrounder*, which provides basic data and facts. For a reference guide to the history and facts about Nasdaq, included is the NASD's monograph, *The Nasdaq Stock Market: Historical Background and Current Operation*. See also Appendix IV, "The NASD/Nasdaq family of Web Sites," which contains facts and extensive statistics on Nasdaq and NASD. Both NASD and Nasdaq web sites feature chronologies of major events throughout their respective histories.

1. *International Encyclopedia of the Stock Market*/Editor: Michael Sheimo. Chicago: Fitzroy Dearborn, 1999. 2 volumes.

Contains entries for terms, people, exchanges, events, etc. listed in one alphabetical sequence. Features entries for "Black Monday," "Backing Away," "Bid Price," "Maloney Act," "National Association of Securities Dealers Automated Quotation System (Nasdaq)," "National Association of Securities Dealers (NASD)," etc. Includes cross-references, indexes of entries, and appendices, which include "Directory of Other Investment Information: Finance, Trade and Banking Organizations." The entry on Nasdaq describes its organization and history.

11

2. Jones-Lee, Anita, Austin Lynas, and Janet Lowe. *Keys to Understanding Securities*. 2nd ed. Barron's Business Keys. Hauppauge, N.Y.: Barron's Educational Series. Inc., 2000. 154 pages.

Introductory work describes basic concepts of securities laws and theories of securities analysis. Provides definitions and explanations of key terms and major legislation. Discusses basic structure, history, and future plans for Nasdaq. Includes annotated guide to online investment resources and a glossary of key terms.

3. *Nasdaq Backgrounder*. Washington, D.C.: Nasdaq, 2000. 25 pages.

Guide to Nasdaq features information on historical background, description of its organization, industry breakdown of Nasdaq companies, Nasdaq indices, Nasdaq market surveillance, listing requirements, directory of Nasdaq and NASD web sites, and frequently asked questions. Includes charts and tables.

4. Pessin, Allan H. and Joseph A. Ross. *The Complete Words of Wall Street: The Professional's Guide to Investment Literacy*. New York: Business One Irwin, 1991. 799 pages.

Dictionary of terms and contains entries for NASDAQ, Level I, Level II, Level III, and the National Association of Securities Dealers (NASD). Cross referenced.

5. Scott, David L. *Wall Street Words: An Essential A to Z Guide for Today's Investor*. Rev. ed. Boston: Houghton, Mifflin, 1998. 433 pages.

Provides entries for terms, agencies, companies, stock exchanges, legislation. Entries provided for NASDAQ, NASDAQ National Market System, NASDAQ OTC Composite Index, NASD, and NASDR. Cross references included.

6. Smith, Jeffrey W., James P. Selway III, and D. Timothy McCormick. *The Nasdaq Stock Market: Historical Background and Current Operation.* NASD Working Paper 98-01. Washington, D.C.: NASD, 1998. 51 pages.

Describes historical developments from the creation of NASD through early 1998. Examines governance and structure of both NASD and Nasdaq and projects future developments. Describes key events in the history of NASD and Nasdaq. For Nasdaq includes description of key legislation and landmark reports, major technological innovations, and the 1994-96 investigations. Includes bibliographical references.

7. Teweles, Richard J. and Edward S. Bradley. *The Stock Market.* 7th ed. New York: John Wiley and Sons, 1998. 568 pages.

Chapter 9 is "The Nasdaq Stock Market and the National Association of Securities Dealers" which contains an overview of the history and organization of NASD and Nasdaq. Discusses Level I, Level II, and Level III services and the Small Order Execution System (SOES). Includes bibliographical references and glossary of terms.

CHAPTER III
BACKGROUND HISTORY

The following sources concern the pre-history of Nasdaq, from the Maloney Act of 1938 to the time prior to the launching of Nasdaq on February 8, 1971. Included in this Chapter are the Maloney Act, a background history of NASD, the 1963 *Special Study of Securities Markets*, a looseleaf service of NASD regulations, and articles released concerning the development of Nasdaq and the recommendations made by the 1963 Special Study.

8. "Bids Solicited on Automated Quote System for Over-the-Counter Prices by the NASD." *Wall Street Journal*, 6 February 1968, p. 5.

Industry sources report that NASD has found an automated quotation system, technically and economically feasible, after a one year study. Estimates by industry sources report that cost to supplier for development and implementation of the system would be $10 million. The one year study was conducted for NASD by Arthur D. Little, Inc. Describes the keystone of the automated system as "a central computer into which market makers would feed bid-and-ask quotations." Additionally, stock salesmen at retail concerns, would have access to median bid-and-ask prices through desk top devices.

15

9. *Federal Securities Laws: Legislative History, 1933-1982.*
   Washington, D.C.: Bureau of National Affairs, 1983. 4 vols.

   Presents legislative history of each statute and amendments thereto, in chronological order. Volume 2 includes text of Securities Exchange Act of 1934, with original legislation and amendments, including Maloney Act. Provides reprint of original texts.

10. Haack, Robert W. "The S.E.C. Special Study and the Over-the-Counter Markets." *Journal of Finance* 21 (May 1966): 333-338.

   Reports changes and proposed changes by NASD in response to the SEC Special Study including implementation of an automated quotations system. The NASD approved the concept of an automated system. Author reports that results of changes, including an automated quotations system, will result in more confidence in the OTC market.

11. Loss, Louis. *Securities Regulation.* 2nd ed. Boston: Little, Brown, 1961. 3 volumes.

   Analyzes securities regulation, including the Maloney Act and organization of the National Association of Securities Dealers. Describes implications of the Maloney Act, appraising it and offering both positive and negative aspects of it. Discusses statutory philosophy and structure of the NASD. Includes extensive bibliographical footnotes.

12. *National Association of Securities Dealers Manual.* Chicago, Illinois: Commerce Clearing House. Looseleaf service.

   Contains: profile of the NASD; roster of former chairmen of the Board of Governors; directory of current officers, committee members, and Board of Governors; directory of Nasdaq officers; directory of NASD Regulation, Inc. officers; district directory; uniform application for broker-dealer registration; list of members; restated certificate of incorporation of NASD; rules of NASD, including general provisions, conduct rules, and membership registration rules; Nasdaq rules; NASD investigations and sanctions; uniform practice code; SEC rules and Regulation T; and code of arbitration procedures. Provides a key word index and is updated by a report letter.

13. "NASD Will Accept Bids from Suppliers to Make Automatic Quote System." *Wall Street Journal*, 19 February 1968, p. 7.

Reports announcement by NASD that it will accept bids from potential suppliers for an automated quotation system for OTC securities. Industry sources reported that NASD has found such a system technically and economically feasible after a one year study.

14. National Association of Securities Dealers, Inc. *History of National Association of Securities Dealers, Inc.: Its Activities, Membership Data, Sanctions Imposed, Members Expelled, Financial Statements, Liaison and Supervision by SEC from 1936 to November 30, 1958.* Printed for the use of the Special Subcommittee on Legislative Oversight of the Committee on Interstate and Foreign Commerce. Washington, D.C.: U.S. Government Printing Office, 1958. 38 pages.

Describes the history and organization of the National Association of Securities Dealers, Inc, which was organized in 1939. NASD is the regulating instrument of the securities business established under the Maloney Act, an amendment to the Securities Act of 1934 (section 15A). The Maloney Act, adopted in 1938, was named for its sponsor Senator Francis T. Maloney of Connecticut. The Maloney Act became law on June 25, 1938. The initial registration of NASD was filed with the SEC on July 20, 1939 and the SEC approved it on August 7. This report describes internal organization of NASD with regard to rules of fair practice; assessments, dues, finances; enforcement of association rules; examination procedure; disciplinary procedures; registered representatives; qualification examination program; uniform practice code; supervision of sales literature; and quotations compiling system for over-the-counter securities. Provides statistical tables covering NASD membership, statement of revenue and expenditures, and registered representatives revoked or suspended from NASD.

15. Robbins, Sidney M., Amyas Ames, and Harry C. Sauvain. "S.E.C.
    Report on the Securities Markets: Discussion." *Journal of Finance*
    21 (May 1966): 339-344.

Comments concerning SEC Special Study by Sidney M. Robbins
of Columbia University, former chief economist of the Special Study;
Amyas Ames of Kidder Peabody; and Harry C. Sauvain of Indiana
University. Describes recommendations of the Special Study and
responses by the exchanges. Sidney Robbins recommends that NASD
pursue automation of the over-the-counter market and comments on the
changes that automation would bring to the market.

16. Simon, Michael J and Robert L.D. Colby. "The National Market
    System for Over-the-Counter Stocks." *George Washington Law
    Review* 55 (November 1986): p. 17-108.

Extensive analysis, from a legal perspective, of the 1963 Special
Study of Securities Markets and actions taken by the SEC to improve
operation of the OTC market. Part I reviews state of OTC market in
1963 and steps taken to implement the recommendations of the 1963
Special Study. Part II discusses SEC's efforts to develop an integrated
national market system and OTC changes brought about. Part III
describes difficulties facing SEC in completing integration of markets
and parallel developments of the OTC market. Reviews origins of
Nasdaq, its organization, and effect on the OTC markets. Discusses
effects of the 1975 Securities Acts Amendments on establishment of the
national market system. Describes recent developments on NASDAQ,
including the elimination of bid-and-ask (RBA) quotation display in
1980 and the implementation of the Small Order Execution System
(SOES) in 1984. Concludes that improvement is needed in areas of
protection of OTC customer orders, handling of limit orders, and sale
of order flow practices. Bibliographical footnotes.

*   Smith, Jeffrey W., James P. Selway III, and D. Timothy
    McCormick. *The Nasdaq Stock Market: Historical Background and
    Current Operation.* see item 6 above.

17. U.S. Congress. Senate. Committee on Banking and Currency. *Regulation of Over-the-Counter Markets...Report to Accompany S. 3255.* 75th Congress, 3rd session. Senate. Report. 1455. Washington, D.C., U.S. Government Printing Office, 1938. 18 pages.

The Maloney Act or Senate bill 3255 amending the Securities Exchange Act of 1934 (by adding section 15A). Aim of amendment is to clarify and strengthen the direct regulatory powers over the over-the-counter markets. Describes the organization of the over-the-counter markets in the United States and discusses the importance of regulation of the over-the-counter markets. Reviews provisions for the over-the-counter markets in the Securities Exchange Act of 1934. Prior to Maloney Act, the over-the-counter markets were dealt with in a brief outline in a single section within the Securities Act of 1934. Proposes a permanent organization for regulation of the over-the-counter markets. Describes NASD's predecessor, the Investment Bankers Conference, Inc. The Maloney Act, sponsored by Senator Francis T. Maloney of Connecticut, formed the basis for establishment of NASD.

18. U.S. Securities and Exchange Commission. *Report of Special Study of Securities Markets of the Securities and Exchange Commission* Washington, D.C.: U.S. Government Printing Office, 1963. 6 volumes in 1.

Reviews SEC legislation and history of the NASD from its establishment in 1938 to 1962-63. Describes role of NASD in governance of the Over-the-Counter Markets. Discusses possibilities of automation of Over the Counter Markets. According to the Special Study, "It seems clear that the kind of automated system described would perform many of the functions of current communication systems and would substantially increase the flow of information about the trading markets to both the professional dealer and the public." (p. 657) The NASD was cited as the natural source of leadership and initiative in dealing with the matter of automation in respect to OTC markets. Landmark study led to establishment of Nasdaq eight years later.

CHAPTER IV
1971-1979

February 8, 1971 marked the first day of operation of Nasdaq, then known as the National Association of Securities Dealers Automated Quotation System or NASDAQ, and several articles listed in Chapter IV relate the story of the first day. The years 1971 through those of 1979 were those of early growth and expansion for this newcomer to securities markets. In the seventies, Nasdaq became the subject of scholarly articles including those by James L. Hamilton, Hans R. Stoll, Seha M. Tinic, and Anthony Santomero. Also included are the hearings for the *Securities Acts Amendments of 1975*, including a follow-up in 1978, that describes NASD's changes in response to the 1975 *Amendments*.

19. Berton, Lee. "NASDAQ: A Three-Year Progress Report." *Financial World* 141 (March 27, 1974): 28-30.

Discusses decline in NASDAQ average trading volume over the past year as well as drop in composite index and lack of companies going public. Reports NASD's optimism about the future of NASDAQ. Regional brokers report positive experiences with NASDAQ. NASD describes various steps taken to increase NASDAQ growth, including discussions with the Federal Reserve to allow more NASDAQ stocks to be purchased on margin; negotiations with the OECD to permit U.S. OTC stocks to be purchased by member OECD nations; and to work with various states' stock regulatory agencies to try to liberalize rules concerning registration of OTC stocks. NASD plans to enhance its computer operations. Concludes that future looks bright for NASD.

20. Bleakley, Fred. "Is NASDAQ Really the Answer?" *Institutional Investor* 4 (July 1971): p. 21-27.

Examines how NASDAQ is working since it was launched in February 1971 and how it is affecting the OTC market. Some 40 market makers, traders and industry regulators were interviewed about NASDAQ. Reports that all is not as smooth as some had hoped. Those interviewed observed greater volatility in the OTC market since launching of NASDAQ. Recommends that more regulation of NASDAQ is needed before an orderly competitive market can be created. States that NASDAQ is still in testing stage and it is premature to draw any final conclusions since NASDAQ has a long way to go before it can be judged as the new central market. States that NASDAQ represents the first step in creation of a central market and is serving an important function.

21. "Clobbering the Stock Exchanges?" *Forbes* 117 (May 15, 1976): 60-61.

Describes how NASDAQ operates and its organizational structure. Reports plans for NASDAQ by Gordon S. Macklin, President of NASD. Macklin plans to have NASDAQ expanded so it will include all NYSE, AMEX, and regional exchange stocks. Additionally, plans are underway for an electronic system that will accept special orders setting a specific price for buying or selling. The system will be called the Consolidated Limit Order Book or CLOB.

22. Eiteman, David K., Charles A. D'Ambrosio, and James C. Van Horne. "Outlook for the Securities Industry: Discussion." *Journal of Financial and Quantitative Analysis* 7 (March 1972): 1702-1705.

Features comments of David K. Eiteman, University of California, Los Angeles; Charles A. D'Ambrosio, University of Washington; and

James C. Van Horne, Stanford University. Eiteman discusses NASDAQ and states that an important consideration in future of stock trading in United States is the existence of competition between stock exchanges as a group and the OTC market. Maintains that a NASDAQ-type system must be allowed to compete with organized exchange-specialist system if stock trading techniques are to become more efficient over a period of years. Observes that spreads are much narrower on NASDAQ. States that he would like to see continued pressure on organized exchanges to innovate with a system similar to NASDAQ's.

23. Goodyear, W. Frederick. "The Birth of NASDAQ." *Datamation* 18 (March 1972): 42-45.

Describes origin of NASDAQ, focusing on computer operations. Describes the Central Processor Complex (CPC) in Trumbull, Connecticut.

24. Hamilton, James L. "Marketplace Organization and Marketability: NASDAQ, the Stock Exchange, and the National Market System. *Journal of Finance* 33 (May 1978): 487-503.

Focuses on the effect of the NASDAQ system on the price of marketability for unlisted common stocks in the OTC marketplace. The term marketability or liquidity of a stock issue means that transactions of its shares are immediately available. Provides a theoretical analysis of marketability in a multidealer marketplace. Compares data before and after implementation of NASDAQ on February 8, 1971. Concludes that empirical analysis of NASDAQ demonstrated that in a multidealer marketplace the prices of marketability are somewhat smaller when dealers use an automated price quotation system. Examines probably effects of a National Market System on prices of marketability for listed stocks. Provides bibliographical references and tables.

25. Hammer, Alexander R. "Counter Market Activates New Quote Unit." *New York Times* 9 February 1971: p. 51+

Reports first day of NASDAQ operation on February 8, 1971.

The new system provides exact up-to-the-minute bid and asked prices on 2400 leading over-the-counter stocks. Describes advantages offered by the new system. Includes interviews with William Turner, assistant director of the NASDAQ Department of NASD and Arthur Dunn, over-the-counter research specialist for G.A. Saxton, Inc. Provides statistical market summary for February 8, 1971.

26. "The Higher Meaning of NASDAQ." *Fortune* 83 (April 1971): 141-144.

Describes the NASDAQ system, in operation since February 1971, featuring a brief account of its history and organization. Discusses immediate benefits of NASDAQ system, its possible long-term effects, and potential rivalry with NYSE and AMEX. Reports NASD Board of Governors approval of proposal on March 13, 1971, to list on NASDAQ 32 NYSE securities and 4 stocks listed on the American and Midwest Exchanges. Features statistical chart comparing OTC and NYSE Average Daily Volume (in shares) from 1967 to the development of NASDAQ.

27. "Journal Today Begins Printing OTC Quotes on New NASD System." *Wall Street Journal,* 9 February 1971, 28.

Announcement that the *WSJ* will begin carrying OTC quotes supplied by the NASDAQ, the new automated quotation system, supervised by NASD. The automated system is starting with about 2150 securities.

28. *NASD and the Listing Dilemma: Factors to be Considered by OTC Companies Contemplating Stock Exchange Listing with NASD.*Washington, D.C.: NASD, 1975. 12 pages

Describes the start of NASDAQ February 8, 1971. Prior to 1971, OTC brokers/dealers relied on telephone and teletype communication. NASDAQ was developed by the National Association of Securities Dealers, Inc., a self-regulatory organization for the over the counter securities market. Reviews how NASDAQ works, cost of listing, and surveillance.

29. "NASD Will Offer Composite Stock Quotes Over Its NASDAQ System by Middle of 1976." *Wall Street Journal* 10 February 1976, p. 3.

Announces NASD's plans to offer, by midyear, a composite stock quotation service over its automated NASDAQ quote system. NASD called this a "second step" toward a central market, following the consolidated transactions tape. NASD formally purchased the NASDAQ system from Bunker Ramo Corporation, which built the system. NASD disclosed it paid approximately $10 million for NASDAQ and will continue to pay about $4 million a year to operate the system for the next four years. Composite quotations service will be available on same terminal on which they currently receive OTC quotes. NASD is considering a "block interest display service," which would display dealer and investor interest in both unlisted and listed large blocks of stock.

30. "NASDAQ Called Peril to American Board; Weeden's Prediction Rebutted by Kolton." *Wall Street Journal* 4 November 1971, p. 6

Relates remarks of Donald E. Weeden, Chairman of Weeden & Co, who predicted that the recently established NASDAQ might bring about the demise of the American Stock Exchange, which he described as an "interim" marketplace. Reports reply from Paul Kolton, President of the American Stock Exchange who reported that public investors and companies will continue to turn increasingly to the American Exchange.

31. "NASDAQ Computing of OTC Stock Volume Delayed Some Months." *Wall Street Journal* 7 June 1971, p. 5.

Reports delay to the investing public in receiving figures on daily trading volume of the 2700 OTC stocks on the NASDAQ. No target date has been reported by NASD for the beginning of the public volume reporting phase of NASDAQ. Reports that NASDAQ was "designed to replace the much criticized market data system still in effect for most over-the-counter stocks, on which published prices are obtained from only one market maker in a stock and volume isn't reported at all."

32. "NASDAQ: Symbol of Change in the Stock Market." *Financial World* 139 (March 28, 1973): p. 4+

Discusses NASDAQ's history, organization, and its impact on the over-the-counter market. NASDAQ is described as a sophisticated, interconnected, electronic communications, network. Contains chart comparing NASDAQ trading activity with activity of NYSE and AMEX.

33. "Power to the NASD!" *Forbes* 110 (October 1, 1972):25-26.

Studies structure of the NASD and discusses how NASDAQ has had a major impact on the OTC market.

34. Reilly, Frank K. *An Early Report Card on the NASDAQ Over-the-Counter Stock Price Indicators.* Research Paper No. 1. Laramie, Wyoming: University of Wyoming, College of Commerce and Industry, 1973.

Analysis of implications of NASD's introducing, on May 17, 1971, a new set of seven stock price indicators. Compares NASDAQ's stock price indicators with NQB (National Quotation Bureau) and with the New York Stock Exchange and the American Stock Exchange. Provides bibliographical references.

35. Santomero, Anthony M. "The Economic Effects of NASDAQ: Some Preliminary Results." *Journal of Financial and Quantitative Analysis* 9 (January 1974): 13-24.

Study examines the economic effects of NASDAQ system on the

Over-the-Counter Market. Investigates success of NASDAQ in making the OTC market a more perfect capital market. Empirical testing involved randomly selected OTC stocks classified by NASD as industrials and listed on NASDAQ. Sample period covered were July 1 to December 30, 1970 and April 1 to September 30, 1971. Focuses on certain aspects of the market, notably spread between bid and ask and cross-price elasticity of substitution between securities and listed stocks to determine if the system has made the market more efficient. Concludes that NASDAQ, given sample set used, has resulted in the efficiency by reducing spreads between bid and ask prices and by reducing price variability from general market trend. Provides statistical tables, bibliographical references, and mathematical formulas used in study.

* Simon, Michael J. and Robert L.D. Colby. "The National Market System for Over-the-Counter Stocks." see item 16 above.

36. Stoll, Hans R. "The Pricing of Dealer Security Services: An Empirical Study of NASDAQ Stocks." *Journal of Finance* 33 (September 1978), 1153-1172.

Using data from NASDAQ from 1973, examines two aspects of dealer behavior that have implications for appropriate structures of securities markets. Study aims to answer questions: 1. What factors determine price of dealer services? and 2. What determines the number of dealers willingly making a market in a stock? A section of this academic study describes the NASDAQ market and presents characteristics of stocks and dealers in the market. Includes statistical tables and bibliographical references.

37. Tellis, Richard I. "How NASDAQ Works." *Public Relations Journal* 17 (June 1971): 13.

Written by Vice President of Doremus and Co., a New York public relations firm which represents NASD and NASDAQ. Discusses beginning of NASDAQ in February 1971 and describes its relationship to NASD. Describes how a company qualifies for NASDAQ and where NASDAQ stocks are listed.

38. *Three Issues in the Development of a Central Securities Market System.* NASD Discussion Paper. Washington, D.C.: National Association of Securities Dealers, Inc., 1976. 39 pages.

Purpose of three part Discussion Paper is to examine several issues which have arisen concerning the development and operation of the national market system. New legislation, the Securities Acts Amendments of 1975 recommend a central, national market system. This Discussion Paper is in three parts and breaks down an effective central market system into three components. Part I, "Sole Self-Regulator Concept" addresses problems of regulatory overlap and suggestions by industry spokesman and Congressional representatives that self-regulatory mechanisms governing the securities industry be streamlined and restructured. Part II, "Potential Uses of NASDAQ Facilities in a Central Market System" studies capabilities and future possible uses of NASDAQ, illustrating how NASDAQ works and how its technology may be integrated into developing a central market system. Part III, "Clearing in a Central Market Environment" discusses the relationship of the clearance function to that of trading and regulatory components of the central market system. Overall purpose of this Discussion Paper is to stimulate discussion, which would lead toward effective use of existing facilities in future restructuring of the securities industry. The section, Part III, is a detailed study of NASDAQ including its history, organization, and non-technical description of the facilities of NASDAQ system. Describes NASDAQ facilities including its Central Processing Complex (CPC) located in Trumbull, Connecticut; trunk lines; Regional Data Concentrators; communications network; control unit; and terminals. Features a simplified diagram of the NASDAQ system. Delineates three phases in the evolution of a central market system for exchange listed securities: Phase 1. Composite Quotations System; Phase 2. Addition to the Composite Quotations System an automatic execution capability with preference for public orders; and Phase 3. A single public book maintained by the System, along with competing market makers and specialists.

39. Tinic, Seha M. "Competition and the Pricing of Dealer Services in the Over-the-Counter Stock Market." *Journal of Financial and Quantitative Analysis* 7 (January 1972): 1707-1727.

Discusses possible effects of changes and developments, including beginning of NASDAQ, on the stock markets. This study provides empirical evidence concerning impact of direct interdealer competition on pricing of dealer services in the OTC market. Principal conclusion is that increase in amount of interdealer competition in this market tend to reduce price of dealer services and therefore, increase marketability of issues. Indicates that growing competition of third market and NASDAQ could have effect of reducing cost of dealer services to buyers and sellers of stocks in the future. Analyzes dealer pricing activity in the OTC market for two periods: 1) day of January 18, 1962 and 2) first five trading days in November 1971. Provides statistical tables and bibliographical references.

40. United States. Congress. Senate. Committee on Banking, Housing, and Urban Affairs. *Securities Acts Amendments of 1975: Hearings before the Subcommittee on Securities of the Commission on Banking, Housing, and Urban Affairs, United States Senate, Ninety-Fourth Congress, First Session on S. 249, To Amend the Securities Exchange Act of 1934, and for other purposes, February 19, 20, and 21, 1975.* Washington, D.C.: U.S. Government Printing Office, 1975. 525 pages.

The objectives of the Securities Acts Amendments of 1975 are to clarify operational direction and regulatory posture of the securities industry, to promote a national market system, and to assure increased competition through competitive commission rates in the securities industry. Includes a statement and testimony by Gordon S. Macklin, President of the National Association of Securities Dealers. Macklin focuses on topics of self regulation and SEC oversight, a national market system for securities, and regulation of municipal securities.

41. United States. Congress. House. Committee on Interstate and Foreign Commerce. Subcommittee on Oversight and Investigations. *Securities Acts Amendments of 1975--Oversight:*

Hearings before the Subcommittee on Oversight and Investigations and the Subcommittee on Consumer Protection, House of Representatives, Ninety-Fifth Congress, First Session: The Functioning and Administration of the Securities Acts Amendments of 1975--National Market System and National Clearance and Settlement System. Washington, D.C.: U.S. Government Printing Office, 1978. 1187 pages.

Provides testimony of Mr. Gordon Macklin, President of the National Association of Securities Dealers. Macklin describes revisions to NASD rules and actions necessitated by the 1975 Securities Acts Amendments. These revisions include: beginning of a Third Market Transaction reporting system in 1975; Consolidated Quotation System through NASDAQ terminals developed in January 1977. A copy of NASD report was submitted describing developments. These included, in addition to the Consolidated Quotations Service, NASDAQ Level II Service to non-NASD members reduced in cost; Combined Consolidated Quotation Service and NASDAQ Level II Service is substantially less expensive than subscribing to both services separately. NASD announced that in mid-1977, subscribers to NASDAQ Level II service will be able to subscribe to NASDAQ options quotations.

CHAPTER V
1980-1986

Materials in this Chapter chronicle the further expansion of Nasdaq, including expansion of its computer facilities, introduction of the National Market System in 1982, implementation of the Small Order Execution System (SOES) in 1984, and beginnings of global expansion. By 1984, Nasdaq became the second largest securities market in the United States.

42. Cooney, John. "The Continuing Appeal of NASDAQ." *Institutional Investor* 18 (February 1984): p. 63+

Reports that more companies are choosing NASDAQ, even though they may qualify for listings on the New York Stock Exchange and the American Stock Exchange. NASDAQ officials report that 600 of its companies could qualify for the NYSE and 1600 for the AMEX. Indicates that NASDAQ is the second largest and fastest growing securities market in the United States. Discusses advantages that NASDAQ has over other exchanges. Reports results of interviews with corporate officers who are listed on NASDAQ and why they stay with NASDAQ and officers who have switched from NASDAQ to another exchange. Describes expansion efforts of NASDAQ including electronic upgrading and increasing companies on its National Market System from 600 to 1600. Interviews NASD President Gordon Macklin.

43. "The Fading Appeal of Listing." *Euromoney* Supplement (March
    1985): 28-31.

Reports that 1800 OTC stocks meet exchange listing criteria, but
choose not to leave NASDAQ. The AMEX or NYSE no longer offered
significantly better visibility to investors. The NYSE and AMEX
reported fewer companies on their list than in 1974, while NASDAQ
has almost twice as many. Interviews company officers who have
chosen not to transfer from NASDAQ. Reports that NASDAQ
popularity has spread overseas and approximately 100 non-U.S.
companies are trading on NASDAQ. Provides graph showing growth
in number of companies on NASDAQ and a table of 100
NASDAQ/NMS market value leaders in 1984.

44. "From Over-the-Counter to Over-the-Computer." *Euromoney*
    Supplement (March 1985): 4-6.

Describes the organization and history of NASDAQ. Charged by
the SEC to organize its members and exploit the new technology,
NASD introduced NASDAQ in 1971. In 1975, as a result of the
Securities Acts Amendments, the SEC directed NASD to include
selected NASDAQ stocks in a national market system. On April 1,
1982, the NASDAQ National Market System began to electronically
relay last trade and volume data on 40 most active NASDAQ stocks.
At the end of 1982, 84 companies were included in the system and by,
1985, 1600 companies have had their stock included in the NASDAQ
NMS. In December 1984, OTC market introduced the Small Order
Execution System (SOES). Dealers can buy and sell small lots (up to
500 shares) at best prices chosen on the screen. Praises efforts of
Gordon Macklin, President of NASD since 1970.

45. Hammer, Alexander R. "OTC Trading: A Busy Field." *New York
    Times* 17 March 1981, p. D2.

Consists of answers to questions asked of Gordon Macklin,
President of NASD, concerning the OTC and Nasdaq. Macklin
comments on reasons for investor interest in OTC stocks, what makes
Nasdaq different from the exchanges, and predictions of growth on

Nasdaq. Macklin states that investors are interested in the bull market for OTC stocks and the fact that many companies traded represent technology and natural resource; Nasdaq differs from other exchanges in that the Nasdaq is a system of competing market makers rather than a single specialist; and that Nasdaq's current growth trend will continue and its volume has already surpassed that of the Amex.

46. "Harris Corp. Gets NASD Job." *Wall Street Journal* 24 April 1980, p. 5.

Announces that Harris Corporation and its data communications division received a $7 million order from NASD to replace 1250 video-display terminals in the offices of brokers, dealers, and financial institutions.

47. Hasbrouk, Joel and Robert A. Schwartz. *The Liquidity of Alternative Marketing Centers: A Comparison of the New York Stock Exchange, the American Stock Exchange, and the NASDAQ National Market System.* American Stock Exchange Data Research Project, 1. New York: American Stock Exchange, 1986.

Explains how markets including NASDAQ work. Maintains that exchange markets are more liquid than the NASDAQ National Market System. Discusses concept of liquidity.

48. "The Institutionalization of NASDAQ." *Forbes* 130 (November 8, 1982): 127.

Describes growth of NASDAQ from 1971 to 1982. NASDAQ accounts for 25% of all shares traded on all exchanges. In 1982, institutions account for 50% of NASDAQ's volume. The number of investors buying NASDAQ stocks doubled from 5 million in 1975 to 10 million in 1980.

49. *Investor Relations: A Practical Guide for NASDAQ Companies.* Washington, D.C.: NASDAQ, 1983. 59 pages.

Results of survey of presidents of NASDAQ companies, institutional investors, individual investors, and registered representatives. Concludes that there is a need for better investor relations and a need to communicate effectively with shareholders about their investments and how to make better investment decisions. Concludes there is need for improved public relations efforts and to work effectively with the press.

50. Loll, Leo M. *The Over the Counter Securities Markets.* 4th ed. Englewood Cliffs, N.J.: Prentice Hall, 1981. 498 pages.

Provides sections explaining history and organization of both NASD and NASDAQ.

51. Macklin, Gordon S. "The NASDAQ Perspective on the World Equity Market: The 24-Hour Global Stock Market." *Vital Speeches of the Day* 52 (January 1, 1986): 168-171.

Transcript of a speech delivered by Gordon S. Macklin, President of the National Association of Securities Dealers, at the Board Meeting of Reuters Holdings, et al., New York City, New York, September 19, 1985. Maintains that the NASDAQ experience in the United States can be replicated successfully internationally. Describes the impact of NASDAQ on the OTC markets, which were fragmented prior to establishment of NASDAQ. Reports that NASDAQ tied OTC market together after its establishment on February 8, 1971. Reports that since 1982, over 2000 NASDAQ companies have joined the NASDAQ National Market System. Describes increase in NASDAQ volume from 1975 to 1984. In 1975, NASDAQ had 21 per cent of total U.S. equity trading and over 28 per cent in 1984. States that NASDAQ is going global and has added 291 ADRs and foreign issues traded in the NASDAQ market. Reports expansion of technologies at NASDAQ including small two-way satellite dishes and the building of the international securities industry first complete back-up market support system.

52. McMurray, Scott. "Amex, NASD Officials Exchange Salvos as Rivalry for Listing of Stocks Heats Up." *Wall Street Journal* 19 February 1984, p. 1.

Reports speech to New York Investors Relations Association by Walter H. Liebman, Amex executive vice president-marketing. Liebman stated that NASD had published "absolute rubbish" resulting in the "misrepresentation and denigration" of exchange trading. States that Gordon Macklin, president of NASD, replied that words from Amex are an expression of Amex's "long term frustration with their loss of market share." Reports that this exchange is latest salvo in continuing rivalry between NASD's Nasdaq and Amex. Controversy based on differences between those who believe in the auction system (practiced by NYSE and Amex) and those who promote multiple market making used over-the-counter (Nasdaq). Compares Nasdaq's growth from 2436 to 3901 listed companies between 1974 to 1983 to declines experienced by NYSE and Amex over same time period. Describes verbal battle between William G. McGowan, a member of NASD's Board of Governors and Walter H. Liebman.

53. McMurray, Scott. "Three Brokerage Firms Moving Toward Automated Over-the-Counter Trading." *Wall Street Journal* 11 January 1985, p. 6.

Reports that three brokerage firms with a major share of the OTC market have installed or will install automated systems to execute trades of up to 1000 shares. These systems enable OTC orders confirmed almost instantaneously. Also reports that Nasdaq's Small Order Execution System (SOES) began in December 1984. SOES provides automated executions for orders of as many as 500 shares.

54. Marsh, Terry and Kevin Rock. *Exchange Listing and Liquidity: A Comparison of the American Stock Exchange with the NASDAQ National Market System.* American Stock Exchange Transactions Data Research Project, Report No. 2. New York, American Stock Exchange, January 1986. 24 pages.

Compares trade-to-trade liquidity of all American Stock Exchange and NASDAQ/NMS common stocks during March and April 1985. Finds absolute value of average trade-to-trade percentage price change is higher for NASDAQ/NMS stocks than for Amex listed stocks of comparable market value, institutional ownership, and long-run price volatility. Amex's advantage is both spreads and intra-quote transactions is attributable to its floor trading and limit order system. Finds the average level of variation in prices of Amex stocks is lower than that of NASDAQ/NMS stocks after controlling for differences in issue size.

55. "NASDAQ Upgrades Facilities, Continuing Bid to Rival NYSE."
    Wall Street Computer Review 2 (May 1985): 15+

    Reports announcement by NASD that it is expanding and updating NASDAQ computer facilities and creating a new backup facility for disaster recovery. NASDAQ trading volume averaged 20 million shares in 1978 and expanded to 60 million shares-per-day by 1984. Upgrade will involve expansion of the central facility in Trumbull, Connecticut. To handle small orders (under 500 shares), the Small Order Execution System (SOES) has been expanded since going online in December 1984. NASDAQ's new capacity is expected to handle 200 million shares-per-day, up from 125 million share capacity.

56. "Over-the-Computer." *Banker* 135 (May 1985): 95+

    Describes growth of NASDAQ that has become the third largest stock exchange in the world, behind New York and Tokyo. Unlike the other exchanges, NASDAQ's center is a warehouse in Trumbull, Connecticut and its trading floor is composed of a network of computers. Reports that NASDAQ launched its National Market System (NMS) in 1982 and in 1981 introduced its Computer Assisted Execution System, to handle off board trading. In December 1984, the Small Order Execution System or SOES was introduced; dealers can trade up to 500 shares at the best prices posted on the screen, without conferring with chosen counterparties. Describes future plans of Gordon Macklin, president of NASD. Among plans are expansion of NMS and SOES.

57. Piontek, Stephen. "NASDAQ Ten Years Old: One Vast Electronic
Stock Market." *National Underwriter (Property-Casualty)* 6 March
1981, p. 4+

Reports celebration in February 1981 of NASDAQ's tenth
anniversary and discusses history and organization of NASDAQ.
Describes growth of NASDAQ during its first decade. In 1980
NASDAQ handled a record 6.69 billion shares, an 83% increase over
1979. At NASD's celebratory luncheon, NASD Chairman L.C.
Peterson stated that from 1975 through 1980, NASDAQ shares traded
had increased at an annually compounded rate of 36.92%. Peterson
predicted further growth in NASDAQ. Gordon Macklin, NASD
President stated that the computer system for NASDAQ will be
upgraded and an automated order execution system will be introduced.
The automated system will allow dealers to handle buy and sell orders
completely by computer.

58. "Policing the Market." *Euromoney* Supplement (March 1985): p.
20-21.

Describes market policing efforts of NASD. Market surveillance
efforts of NASD include examining trading patterns of all firms trading
in the market. When activity in a security breaks any of its parameters,
the alarm goes off in the Market Surveillance section. There are 6000
parameter breaks a year. The Market Surveillance Committee, which
reports to the NASD Board of Governors, provides disciplinary action.
Relates efforts of NASD examiners located in District Offices. When
District Committees find violations, they impose penalties on firms and
individuals, including Letters of Caution, suspension, or possible
expulsion. Article features comments by Peter Byrne, 1985 Chairman
of the NASD Board and Chris Franke, in charge of Market
Surveillance.

59. "The Power behind NASDAQ." *Banker* 135 (May 1985): p. 95.

Discusses computer infrastructure of NASDAQ, including the
major computer center in Trumbull, Connecticut and systems at
NASDAQ's administrative headquarters in Washington, D.C.

60. "Presiding Over Change." *Euromoney* Supplement (March 1985): 10-15.

Series of interview questions answered by Gordon Macklin, President of NASD since 1970. Macklin answers questions related to expansion efforts for NASDAQ; his career experience before he came to NASD; his work in overseeing the development of NASDAQ from the time it was under construction in 1970; his comments on the impact of NASDAQ; expansion to a global marketplace; and the introduction of the NASDAQ National Market System.

61. Putka, Gary. "NASD Agrees to Price Link with Britain: Quotes on up to 580 Stocks will be Shared in Plan with London Exchange." *Wall Street Journal* 26 November 1985, p. 1.

Reports that the London Stock Exchange and the NASD agreed to swap price quotation information on as many as 580 stocks. This move would enable U.S. investors to see prices of as many as 300 London traded stocks on the Nasdaq system.

62. Sloan, Allan, with Aaron Bernstein. "NASDAQ Goes Upscale." *Forbes* 128 (December 28, 1981), p. 31 +

Describes efforts by NASDAQ to upgrade its image. The NASD removed the penny stocks out of most daily newspapers and substituted larger and more respectable companies. To make the national list, a company must meet certain financial criteria, including market value, net worth, number of years in business, and profitability. Gordon Macklin, President of NASD, stated that changes were made to decrease volatility of the NASDAQ national list.

63. Stewart, Scott Dudley. *Price Adjustment on the NASDAQ Market: A Thesis presented to the Faculty of the Graduate School of Cornell University in partial fulfillment for the Degree of Doctor of Philosophy, June 1985*. Ann Arbor, Michigan: University Microfilms International, 1986. 150 pages.

Describes characteristics of NASDAQ, including its being characterized by both publication of bid and asked quotes instead of transaction prices and very few regulations interfering with the price adjustment mechanism. Explains ways NASDAQ differs from the other exchanges. This empirical study focuses on the seasonality in the NASDAQ market and examines quotation returns. Reviews previous studies of the literature. Study recognizes that the use of bid and asked quotes may introduce more statistical noise than transaction prices. Provides history of development of NASDAQ. Includes bibliographical references.

64. "Trading on Chips." *Euromoney* Supplement (March 1985): p. 6-10.

Detailed report on NASDAQ's technology. Describes the main computer center in Trumbull, Connecticut which has grown from two computers and a handful of staff in 1971 to over 30 mainframes and a payroll of over 300 people in 1985. Over 120,000 terminals worldwide receive data that has been processed in Trumbull. Interviews Frank Coyle, Vice-President in charge of systems operation at the site outside Trumbull. Reports NASDAQ's acquiring the right to purchase its computer system from Bunker Ramo in February 1976. By 1981 Bunker Ramo terminals were replaced by more advanced machines built by Harris Corporation. The NASD is looking toward building an alternative processing center outside of Washington, D.C. Aims to allow traders to adjust live price data constantly on their NASDAQ terminals. Includes statistical chart tracking the growth in NASDAQ quotations terminals.

CHAPTER VI
1987-1994

This time period was a pivotal one for Nasdaq, the year 1987 being the year of the October Crash and 1994 the start of one of the most challenging events in Nasdaq's history. Included in this chapter are the *Brady Commission Report*, which discussed the problem of market makers not answering phones and effectively leaving the market during the October Crash. NASD's resultant changes in rules are described in several articles in this chapter. Several articles profile NASD Chief Executive Officer Joseph Hardiman and describe his role in fostering improvements on Nasdaq during the late 1980s and early 1990s. Additional reforms and changes to Nasdaq would be triggered by a news release in May 1994, describing the findings in an forthcoming scholarly article by William Christie of Vanderbilt University and Paul Schultz of Ohio State University. Their findings revealed that Nasdaq market makers avoided odd-eighths quotes and suggested collusion among these market makers to increase spreads or trading profits. This triggered lawsuits and investigations, about which more will be written in the next Chapter.

It should be noted here, that Nasdaq, in 1990 became formally known as the Nasdaq Stock Market, instead of NASDAQ (National Association of Securities Dealers Automated Quotation System). Authors of materials written 1990 and later, with few exceptions, now refer to the market as Nasdaq.

65. "American Stockmarkets: Against the Odds." *Economist* 332 (August 20, 1994): 59.

Reports the filing of more than 20 lawsuits that accuse securities dealers of price-fixing. The lawsuits started after publication of the Christie-Schultz study findings in the May 27, 1994 *Los Angeles Times*.

66. Blanton, Kim. "Study Claims Nasdaq Dealers Set Prices to Enhance Profits." *Boston Globe* 27 May 1994, p. 86.

Describes implications of study by William Christie and Paul Schultz, suggesting Nasdaq dealers may be involved in "tacit collusion" to increase trading profits or spreads. Christie-Schultz study found that 71 percent of 100 actively traded stocks, including Apple Computer and Lotus Development Corp. were not priced at odd-eighths. According to Christie, he and Schultz were "careful to say in the study we don't know if they are colluding." But, "the persistent lack of odd-eights trades is very unusual and difficult to explain where up to 50 dealers are competing for order flow." Blanton article reports initial, negative reaction from Nasdaq, in form of statement by its spokesman, Robert Ferri.

67. Christie, William G, Jeffrey H. Harris, and Paul H. Schultz. "Why did Nasdaq Market Makers Stop Avoiding Odd-Eighth Quotes?" *Journal of Finance* 49 (December 1994): 1841-1860.

Examines the sudden increase in odd-eighth quotes by market dealers including Lotus Development, Cisco Systems, Microsoft, and Apple Computer, after national newspapers released findings of the Christie and Schultz study on May 26 and 27 1994. This academic study maintains that "it is difficult to understand why, in a competitive market, over 40 dealers simultaneously changed a pricing practice that had been effect for years only after the practice was made public." Contains bibliographic references, tables, and statistical figures.

68. Christie, William G. and Paul H. Schultz. "Why do Nasdaq Market
    Makers Avoid Odd-Eighth Quotes." *Journal of Finance* 49
    (December 1994): 1813-1840.

Highly influential academic paper and the major catalyst for
reform finds that odd-eighth quotes are virtually nonexistent for 70 of
100 traded Nasdaq securities. This also led to follow-up academic
research studies refuting or agreeing with the implications of collusion.
Implies a $.25 inside spread among Nasdaq stocks, raising questions
of Nasdaq dealers' implicit collusion to maintain wide spreads. Results
of this study were released to several national newspapers triggering
legal action and investigations by the SEC, the U.S. Department of
Justice, and the Rudman Committee. Studies extensive sample of inside
bid and inside ask quotes for 100 of most active NASDAQ stocks in
1991. Nasdaq firms studied trade on the National Market System
(NMS). Compares Nasdaq stocks to 100 NYSE/AMEX stocks of
comparable price and end of year equity value. Bibliography, tables,
and statistical figures.

69. Cochran, Thomas N. "The Striking Price: The Last Hundred
    Years?" *Barron's* 1 August 1994, p. MW10.

Reports that antitrust suits were filed in California, Illinois, the
District of Columbia, and New York, the suit naming many of the
largest OTC market makers. Suits came as a result of the yet
unpublished Christie-Schultz study, with implied collusion among
market makers.

70. Donlan, Thomas G. "Crash Course in Market Reform: Next Time
    OTC Dealers Will Answer Their Phones." *Barron's* 18 July
    1988, p. 13+

Discusses ramifications of Nasdaq market makers leaving phones
off the hook during October 1987 Crash. Describes NASD's new rules
which require members to continue executing orders in face of large
sell-off. Also, it is now required that market makers participate in
Nasdaq's automated execution system (SOES). Reports reaction to
changes by several market makers.

71. Fortin, Richard D., R. Corwin Grube, and O. Maurice Joy.
    "Seasonality in NASDAQ Dealer Spreads." *Journal of Financial
    and Quantitative Analysis* 24 (September 1989): 395-407.

    Examines seasonal behavior of proportional dealer spreads for
    OTC NASDAQ common stocks. Sample studied was NASDAQ
    historical data file prepared by the Center for Research in Security
    Prices (CRSP) from January 1, 1973 through December 31, 1985.
    Results indicate there is a seasonality in dealer spreads; these spreads
    tend to be larger in the second half of the year, with peak in December.
    At the turn of the year, spreads tend to peak in mid to late December
    and recede in January. The largest daily decline in spreads during the
    turn of the year period is on the last trading day in December. Includes
    statistical tables and bibliographical references.

72. Getler, Warren and William Power. "Small Stock Focus: Nasdaq
    Critic Vows He isn't taking sides." *Wall Street Journal* 21
    November 1994, p. C1+

    In an interview with William Christie, finance professor at
    Vanderbilt University, who co-wrote 1994 study maintains that he and
    Schultz are not taking sides. Christie maintains that specific problems
    concerning Nasdaq needed to be addressed. Christie reports that if he
    were an active investor, he would have no problem trading on Nasdaq.
    Paul Schultz, in an interview reported that the odd-eighth quotes was
    something that he and Christie did not expect to find. Christie
    maintains that he is not taking sides in the various cases and
    investigations, but is willing to discuss his findings with interested
    parties. Christie is planning a study on tightening of the spread in Intel
    Corporation. Christie reports that he is receiving major attention from
    the news media regarding the study.

73. Karpoff, Jonathan M. and Ralph A. Walkling. "Dividend Capture
    in NASDAQ Stocks." *Journal of Financial Economics* 28
    (November-December 1990): 39-65.

    Examines importance of dividend capture trading in NASDAQ
    stocks by testing for cross-sectional relations between ex-day abnormal

returns and bid-ask spreads. Dividend capture is defined as practice of buying a stock shortly before its ex-dividend day and selling it soon after. Reviews previous research studies on dividend-capture hypothesis. Studies sample of NASDAQ stocks traded from 1973-1985. Finds that ex-day returns and spreads are positively related. Findings indicate that dividend-capture trading affects the ex-day returns of at least some, especially high yield NASDAQ stocks and that dividend capture trading is important for understanding ex-dividend day returns.

74. Lamoreaux, Christopher G. and Gary C. Sanger. "Firm Size and Turn-of-the-Year Effects in the OTC/NASDAQ Market." *Journal of Finance* 44 (December 1989): 1219-1245.

Empirical study examines the turn-of-the-year effect, firm size effect and relationship between the two effects for an example of OTC stocks traded on NASDAQ from January 1, 1973 through December 31, 1985. Reviews previous studies in the literature. Paper contains: description of data set and methodology; presentation of evidence on size effect for NASDAQ stocks; examination of interaction between firm size and seasonality of returns; consideration of daily returns and trading characteristics surrounding turn-of-the-year; and study of interrelationships among firm size, return, and bid-ask spreads. Includes parallel results for NYSE and AMEX stocks over same sample period, with same methodology. Concludes that small firms tend to earn significant, positive abnormal returns in January and conversely, for larger firms. General results are not sensitive to changes in composition of market index. Contains statistical tables and bibliographic references.

75. Lewis, Kate Bohner. "Juicy Spreads." *Forbes* 154 (September 26, 1994): 14.

On August 16, 1993, *Forbes* had reported that securities brokers have pushed Nasdaq stocks since the Nasdaq market offers larger spreads for brokers. Allegation was rebutted by the NASD and brokers. William Christie and Paul Schultz have prepared a study indicating that Nasdaq market makers keep Nasdaq bid and ask spreads at $.25 or more.

76. Lockwood, Larry J. and Scott C. Linn. "An Examination of Stock Market Return Volatility During Overnight and Intraday Periods, 1964-1989." *Journal of Finance* 45 (June 1990): 591-601.

Examines variance of hourly market returns during 1964-1989. Results indicate that market variance is shown to change significantly over time: rising after the introduction of NASDAQ (1971); rising after standardized stock options (1973); falling after negotiable commissions (1975); rising after stock index futures (1982); and falling after increased margin requirements for trading in stock index futures (1988). Includes statistical tables and bibliographical references.

77. Lux, Hal. "Wall Street on Trial." *Investment Dealers Digest* 1 August 1994, p. 16+

Relates that William Christie and Paul Schultz began gathering data in 1993 for a study of liquidity on the Nasdaq Stock Market. They studied the volatile trading day, November 15, 1991 and discovered that they could not find odd-eighth quotes for large majority of Nasdaq stock sales; they only found even ones such as two-, four-, and six-eighth. Christie and Schultz studied a larger number of Nasdaq quotations, still not discovering odd-eighth quotes for most stocks. Their findings were written up in the 1994 article, "Why do Nasdaq Market Makers Avoid Odd-Eighth Quotes." Results of their study were disclosed in a May 26, 1994 story in the *Los Angeles Times*. After the story's release, Christie and Schultz received numerous calls from lawyers requesting copies of their study. Reporters also called the co-authors. Lux reports that within the past two months, every major OTC market maker, including Goldman, Sachs & Co. and Merrill Lynch, were served with papers alleging price-fixing, antitrust violations, collusion and fraud. Additionally, the U.S. Department of Justice's Antitrust Division contacted Christie and Schultz requesting a copy of their article. Lux reports initial reactions from Nasdaq market makers, who are "concerned but not panicked" by the lawsuits. Speculation is offered by Nasdaq market makers and attorneys as to the outcome of the lawsuits.

78. "The Man Who Would Make Securities More Secure." *Business Week* 3061 (July 18, 1988): 124.

Profiles Joseph Hardiman, CEO of NASD, who dealt with the effects of the October 1987 stock market crash. During the crash, the market went into a free fall and NASD market makers did not answer phones, ducking orders. Hardiman initiated a series of reforms, including mandatory participation by market makers in the Small Order Execution System (SOES). Market makers also can no longer withdraw when markets are volatile. Hardiman plans to investigate trading abuses including unauthorized trading and embezzlement of customer funds. Reports that Hardiman sees his job as rebuilding investor confidence through an increase in enforcement measures.

79. *Market 2000: An Examination of Current Equity Market Developments*/U.S. Securities and Exchange Commission. Division of Market Regulation. Washington, D.C.: U.S. Securities and Exchange Commission, Division of Market Regulation, For sale by the Superintendent of Documents, U.S. Government Printing Office, 1994. 1 volume (various paging).

Studies structure of the U.S. securities markets, including Nasdaq. States that the principles in the Securities Acts Amendments of 1975 provide rationale for proposals for action recommended in this study. Recommends improvements in four areas: 1. Fair treatment of investors; 2. Market information provided in timely and comprehensive manner; 3. Fair competition among markets and market participants; 4. Expansion of open market access. Regarding Nasdaq, recommends improving order handling practices for securities quoted and improving overall quality of the OTC market. Reviews trends in the securities markets over the past 20 years. Provides bibliographic references, tables, and charts.

80. Morgenson, Gretchen. "Fun and Games on Nasdaq." *Forbes* 152 (August 16, 1993): 74+

Studies Nasdaq growth and maintains that Nasdaq volume is more profitable for brokers than investors. Since it is more profitable for brokers, they are given more incentive to promote Nasdaq stocks. Explains Nasdaq growth and its outgrowing the New York Stock Exchange. Compares Nasdaq organization to those of NYSE and AMEX. Investors do not benefit since they often must pay higher spreads.

81. "The NASD: A Computerized Mouse that's Roaring." *Business Week* 3178 (February 17, 1990): 128-129.

Reports new developments on the Nasdaq, including plans to expand to include more companies in the U.S. and overseas. Discusses an increasing number of companies staying with Nasdaq and not moving to other exchanges. Describes reforms by NASD's Joseph Hardiman including increasing penalties for dealers who deserted their terminals during a sell-off. Concludes that, for Nasdaq, the future is now.

82. *The NASDAQ Handbook: The Stock Market of Tomorrow--Today: A Complete Reference for Investors, Registered Representatives, Company Executives, Researchers, the Financial Press, and Students of Finance.* Chicago: Probus Publishing Co., 1987. 577 pages.

Series of essays on the NASDAQ. Organized into parts: Pt. 1. "America's Fastest Growing Stock Market"; Pt. 2. "NASDAQ Companies: Who are they?"; Pt. 3. "The Investors"; Pt. 4. "The Brokers and Dealers in NASDAQ Stocks"; Pt. 5. "NASDAQ as an Economic Institution"; and Pt. 6. "The Financial Media Look at NASDAQ"; and Pt. 7. "The NASDAQ System: Services and Regulations." Describes origins and history of NASDAQ and NASD. Features glossary and bibliography.

83. *The Nasdaq Handbook: The Stock Market for the Next 100 Years: A Complete Reference for Investors, Registered Representatives, Company Executives, Researchers, the Financial Press, and Students of Finance.* Chicago: Probus Publishing Co., 1992. 388 pages.

Series of essays on Nasdaq. Organized into parts: Pt. 1. "America's Fastest Growing Stock Market"; Pt. 2. "Nasdaq Companies: Who are They"; Pt. 3. "Investing in Nasdaq"; Pt. 4. "Market Making: Where Competition and Technology Meet"; Pt. 5. "Nasdaq as a National Economic Institution." Describes history of Nasdaq and NASD. Provides glossary and bibliography.

84. National Association of Securities Dealers, Inc. *Final Report of the Regulatory Review Task Force.* Washington, D.C.: NASD, March 1988. 42 pages.

Report of Task Force appointed by NASD President, Gordon S. Macklin. Task Force reviewed NASD regulatory programs for purpose of making recommendations to improve their effectiveness. Study discussed need to survey the market to watch for insider trading schemes. Studied market surveillance techniques, its history and background. Task Force recommendations included NASD's refining real time stockwatch parameters and changing the language of the Nasdaq listing agreement to require notification to the Nasdaq Market Surveillance Section at least ten minutes before news is released to the media.

85. National Association of Securities Dealers. *NASD: Fifty Years of Helping Make America Strong.* Washington, D.C.: NASD, 1989. 16 pages.

Commemorates NASD's 50th Anniversary. Reviews history of NASD and describes organization of NASD and Nasdaq Stock Market. Provides timeline of major events in NASD and Nasdaq.

86. National Association of Securities Dealers. Special Committee on NASD Structure and Governance. *Report of the Special Committee on NASD Structure and Governance.* Washington, D.C.: NASD, 1990.

Review of structure and governance of NASD in light of great changes that have occurred in the securities markets and in the industry serving those markets. Provides brief history of the NASD. In May 1989, the NASD Special Committee began review of the corporate structure of NASD and its subsidiaries, including Nasdaq. Recommends that NASD continue direct oversight of the Nasdaq, but states improvements could be made in governance of Nasdaq and in the ability of the NASD and its subsidiaries to respond to intensified competition. Recommends that no changes should be made to basic corporate structure of the NASD and its subsidiaries at this time.

87. Paltrow, Scot J. "Is This a Fair Trade?" *Los Angeles Times* 21 October 1994, p. D1 +

The second in series of Paltrow's "Inside Nasdaq." Presents case studies of small investors whose customer orders of Nasdaq stocks were ignored. Cases of "trading through" or ignoring customer orders are examined. "Trading through" ensures large profits for market makers at expense of investors. Contains glossary of terms and graph illustrating growth of Nasdaq in the 1990s.

88. Paltrow, Scot J. "Nasdaq: Study Suggests Market Rigging." *Los Angeles Times* 16 May 1994, p. D1 +

Describes results of academic study by William Christie and Paul Schultz. Copies of their report were made available on Wednesday, May 25, 1994. The paper was accepted by the *Journal of Finance* for publication in about six months. The stock data examined Nasdaq stock data and found that the majority of the stocks almost never are posted in "odd-eighth." Profit the brokerage firm was almost never less than a quarter of a point or $.25 per share. Collusion is strongly suggested among nation's brokerage houses. Paltrow's article reports reaction by Richard G. Ketchum, chief operating officer of the NASD. Reactions of NASD were negative. Several brokerage firms, including Merrill Lynch, Prudential Securities, and Smith Barney Shearson offered no comment or did not respond to calls asking for comments. Initial news reports, including this article, triggered immediate response in form of lawsuits and major investigations.

89. Paltrow, Scot J. "The Price of Backing Away." *Los Angeles Times* 23 October 1994, p. D1+

Fourth in series, "Inside Nasdaq." Reports allegations that Nasdaq market makers often do not honor the "firm quote rule," requiring market makers to honor prices they display. Instead they "backed away" from their obligation to trade at posted prices. Newspaper investigation found on visiting trading desks, about two dozen cases of "backing away." Reports interview with James M. Cangiano, NASD Executive Vice President for Market Surveillance who contended majority of "backing away" complaints, frivolous. Contains glossary of terms.

90. Paltrow, Scot J. "Probe Launched into Nasdaq Stock Trading." *Los Angeles Times* 19 October 1994, p. A1+

Announces the Justice Department's opening an antitrust investigation of the Nasdaq stock market, specifically allegations of price fixing and other illegal practices. Follows May release of Christie-Schultz findings.

91. Paltrow, Scot J. "Pros Say Many Nasdaq Trades Reported Late." *Los Angeles Times* 24 October 1994, p. D1+

Fifth in series, "Inside Nasdaq." Reports some Nasdaq trade reports come in 90 seconds after their execution. Delays in trade only allowed in events of glitch or trading ticket lost. Alleges "painting the tape" or delaying trade reports among some Nasdaq market makers. This is evident among some traders in pension and mutual funds. Shows computer report of Nasdaq trading in shares of Microsoft, Inc.

92. Paltrow, Scot J. "Revised System for Small Lot Trades Decried as Unfair." *Los Angeles Times* 22 October 1994, p. D1+

Third in a series, "Inside Nasdaq." Describes effects of October 1987 crash on Nasdaq. During crash, Nasdaq dealers stopped trading and individual investors could not sell. SOES or Small Order Execution System was established on Nasdaq after the Crash to execute orders automatically without investors needing to call market makers. Current reports are that NASD will scale down SOES and possibly eliminate it. Replacement system described is N-Prove System, favored by large market makers. Small investors have complained to SEC regarding this possible change.

93. Paltrow, Scot J. "SEC Launches Probe of Nasdaq Trading Activity." *Los Angeles Times* 15 November 1994, p. A1+

Reports the SEC's launching of a review of the Nasdaq Stock Market, investigating allegations of possible collusion. This represents the first major investigation of an entire stock market's operations since the SEC's investigation of the American Stock Exchange in the 1960s.

94. Paltrow, Scot J. "Taking Stock of Nasdaq." *Los Angeles Times* 20 October 1994, p. A1+

The first in Paltrow's series, "Inside Nasdaq," examines recent allegations of collusion. Consists of interviews with Nasdaq market makers and the NASD President who comment on the allegations. Contains "Glossary of Common Terms Used on Nasdaq" and statistical tables, including illustration charting impact of Nasdaq "spreads." Compares organization of Nasdaq with other exchanges including the New York Stock Exchange.

95. Paltrow, Scot J. "Vigilance is Still the Watchword." *Los Angeles Times* 25 October 1994, p. D1+

Sixth in series, "Inside Nasdaq." Presents ways in which small investors can protect themselves in the OTC markets, including Nasdaq. Advice includes: investing in mutual funds instead of directly buying Nasdaq stock and buying and holding Nasdaq stock for the long-term and discouraging short-term holding. Indicates possibility of Nasdaq reform in light of Justice Department and SEC investigations.

96. Reiganum, Marc R. "Market Microstructure and Asset Pricing: An Empirical Investigation of NYSE and NASDAQ Securities." *Journal of Financial Economics* 28 (November-December 1990: 127-147.

Investigates influence of market microstructure on liquidity premiums. Contrasted are premiums of a competitive, multi-dealer market (NASDAQ) and those of a monopolistic, specialist system (NYSE). Differences in liquidity premiums are estimated from monthly stock returns. Findings indicate: 1) Among small firms, average returns of NYSE securities exceed average returns of similar-sized NASDAQ securities; 2) return differential between NASDAQ and NYSE securities decreases as stock market centralization increases; and 3) among similar sized small firms, return differentials between NASDAQ and NYSE securities persists after controlling for various risk and liquidity-related measures. Includes statistical tables and bibliographical references.

*   Simon, Michael J. and Robert L.D. Colby. "The National Market System for Over-the-Counter Stocks." see item 16 above.

97. Sofianos,   George.   *A   Comparison   of   Market   Making Structures.* Federal Reserve Bank of New York. Research Paper, No. 8821. New York: Federal Reserve Bank of New York, September 1988. 29 leaves.

Examines and compares main market making features of: the New York Stock Exchange, the NASDAQ/Over-the-Counter-Market, London's International Stock Exchange, and Tokyo's Stock Exchange. Three features are examined: market making obligations, market making capital, and order flow arrangements. Study briefly examines market design in general, and then, each market in turn. Discusses implications of 1987 Crash. Provides bibliographical references and tables.

98. "Spread 'em." *Economist* 333 (November 5, 1994): 81.

Reviews implications of Christie and Schultz study (1994) alleging collusion. Recommends follow-up and need for more studies.

99. Trivoli, George W. and Siva P. Uppala. *Testing the Relative Efficiency of the NYSE, AMEX and Nasdaq by   Measuring Bid/Ask Spreads.* CCBA Working Paper No. 9. Jacksonville, Alabama: Jacksonville State University, College of Commerce and Business Administration, November 1994.

Study focuses on the relative efficiency of NYSE, AMEX, and Nasdaq as measured by bid-ask spreads. The basic presumption of this study is that the greater the bid-ask spread for actively traded stocks, other things being equal, the lesser the efficiency of the specific market. In other words, the market in which the spread tends to be greater, the market will be less efficient of competitive. Studies intraday trades and quotations for the three exchanges. Finds that there are: 1) significant differences between bid-ask spreads on NYSE, AMEX, and Nasdaq; 2) differences in price, volume, and capitalization all contribute to the variability of bid-ask spreads; 3)the least efficient markets appear to be regional exchanges trading both NYSE and AMEX stocks; and 4) there appears to be a definite trend in all markets tested over the period toward a shrinkage of bid-ask spreads. This study fails to support contention that there is apparent collusion among broker dealers in the Nasdaq market as indicated in the Christie-Schultz 1994 study. Provides bibliographical references and statistical tables.

100. U.S. General Accounting Office. *Financial Markets: Stronger System Controls and Oversight Needed to Prevent   NASD Computer Outages: Report to the Chairman and Ranking Minority Member, Subcommittee on   Telecommunications and Finance, Committee on Energy and Commerce, House of Representatives.* Washington, D.C.: General Accounting Office; For sale by the U.S. Government Printing Office, December 1994. 1 vol. (various paging).

Report responds to August 2, 1994 letter requesting review of recent outages experiences by Nasdaq. Report determines: nature and cause of the outages of July 14, 15, and August 1, 1994; the impact of the outages on market participants; adequacy of NASD's approach to respond to contingencies and disasters; how well NASD oversees its automated systems and facilities; and how well the SEC is ensuring preparedness of securities markets in the event of contingencies and disasters. Reports that respective outages were caused by unrelated software and hardware malfunctions. Calls for further improvement in SEC's oversight programs. Recommends that NASD: expands testing processes for market systems; assesses existing systems thoroughly to identify weaknesses; avoid implementing changes in software on potentially volatile trading days; corrects weaknesses in its contingency and disaster recovery plan and backup data processing facility; and regularly schedules and conducts audits of its market systems.

101. U.S. General Accounting Office. *Financial Markets: Tighter Computer Security Needed: Report to the Chairman, Subcommittee on Telecommunications and Finance, Committee on Energy and Commerce, House of Representatives.* Washington, D.C.: General Accounting Office; For sale by the Superintendent of Documents, U.S. Government Printing Office, January 1990. 1 vol. (various paging)

Studies computer security in various systems including the common message switch system and the Intermarket Trading System operated by the Securities Industry Automation Corporation and the Nasdaq System. Examines the number of known cases of hacker attempts or virus attacks. Recommends that the SEC: 1. Ensures that weaknesses found in the system are properly corrected; 2. oversee the exchanges' and NASD's plans to expand their information security programs; 3. conduct or oversee assessments of the exchanges' and NASD's computer security practices; and 4. acquire the necessary technical expertise to carry out these activities. Regarding NASD, study found insufficient internal controls to protect against the introduction of security intrusions such as a virus, into the NASDAQ system. Internal control weaknesses had been discussed with NASD officials who agreed to move swiftly to improve their controls and their system.

102. U.S. Presidential Task Force on Market Mechanisms. *Report of the Presidential Task Force on Market Mechanisms.* New York: The

Task Force, For Sale by the Superintendent of Documents, U.S. Government Printing Office, Washington, D.C., 1988. 1 vol. (various paging).

Section of this report, more commonly known as the Brady Commission Report, describes effects of the October 1987 Crash on Nasdaq. During the week of October 19, 1987 some Nasdaq market makers formally withdrew from making markets and did not answer phones. Includes statistical chart of Nasdaq market activities from 10/15/87 through 10/21/87. During this time period, bid and ask spreads widened. Reports that NASD took swift and dramatic action and on November 13, 1987 at a NASD Board meeting, amendments were proposed for rules of practice and procedure for SOES. Proposed amendments included: prohibiting a firm that has withdrawn on an unexcused basis as a Nasdaq market maker from re-entering Nasdaq as a market maker in that security for 30 days; limiting the acceptable reasons for excused withdrawal to physical circumstances (equipment malfunction, etc.), participating in SOES is mandatory for all market makers in each of the NMS securities in which they make quotes in Nasdaq; enabling NASD to establish different levels of maximum order size limits for SOES orders; and eliminating preferencing of market makers during locked or crossed market situation.

CHAPTER VII
1995-2000

During the time period 1995 through mid-2000 many critical events took place in the history of Nasdaq. The ramifications of the Christie Schultz 1994 study were investigations by the SEC and the U.S. Department of Justice, as well as lawsuits. Settlement of the lawsuits and results of U.S. Justice Department investigations were made in 1996 and major reports were written by the SEC and by NASD, through its "Rudman Report." The NASD, SEC, and U.S. Department of Justice reports have been included in this chapter, only with press accounts of the investigations. Articles and reports detailing subsequent reforms of NASD and Nasdaq are contained in this chapter. Additionally, scholarly articles and working papers were written during this time period, some agreeing with and others refuting the implications of collusion described in the Christie-Schultz study. These include scholarly articles and working papers by Dean Furbush, Allan Kleidon, Robert D. Willig, Merton Miller, and Sanford J. Grossman.

Advances by Nasdaq during this time period included establishment of the MarketSite; the merger with the Amex Stock Market; and further global expansion into Europe and Asia. During the first part of 2000, the forthcoming decimalization of Nasdaq would take place in 2001 and a new system, Super Montage was announced.

103. Baker, Molly. "Nasdaq Fights Back on Pricing Allegations." *Wall Street Journal* 5 April 1995, p. C1.

Reports that Nobel Laureate, Merton Miller will present response at a Vanderbilt University, Financial Market's Research Center conference, on behalf of Nasdaq, to the 1994 Christie-Schultz study. Reports that when results of study first came out in May 1994, Nasdaq officials were slow to respond, then played down the study. Miller maintains charges made in Christie-Schultz study drew false conclusions regarding charges of collusion among Nasdaq market makers. Dean Furbush of Economists Incorporated will also present a study on behalf of Nasdaq. Another study defending Nasdaq will be presented by Allan W. Kleidon of Stanford University Law School and Robert D. Willig of Princeton University.

104. Barclay, M. "Bid-Ask Spreads and the Avoidance of Odd-Eighth Quotes on Nasdaq: An Examination of Exchange Listings." *Journal of Financial Economics* 45 (July 1997): 9-34.

Examines the relation between bid-ask spreads and the avoidance of odd-eighth quotes on Nasdaq. Reviews Christie and Schultz (1994) point of view and alternative view that high spreads observed on Nasdaq reflect high market making costs for Nasdaq securities. This study attempts to discriminate between these views by studying 472 securities that were listed on Nasdaq and moved to NYSE or Amex between 1983 and 1992. Compares effect of exchange listing on securities for which Nasdaq market makers avoided odd-eighth quotes with effect on securities for which market makers used both odd and even eighths. While on Nasdaq, securities for which market makers showed larger bid and ask spreads than securities for which market makers used both odd and even eighths. Offers three potential explanations for observations that bid-ask spreads are higher on Nasdaq than on NYSE: 1. Spreads on Nasdaq are competitive and reflect higher cost of market making for Nasdaq securities; 2. Spreads on Nasdaq are supra-competitive due to inefficient market structure or institutional practices that suppress incentives for price competition and 3. Spreads on Nasdaq are supra-competitive because of collusion among Nasdaq market makers. Concludes that bid-ask spreads fall when securities move from Nasdaq to NYSE or Amex and that large differences in effective spreads between securities for which market makers avoid odd-eighths quotes and those for which market makers use both odd and even eighths is nearly eliminated when same securities are traded on NYSE or Amex. Results indicate that avoidance of odd-eights quotes is used as a coordination device among Nasdaq market makers to increase bid-ask spreads to supra-competitive levels. Provides bibliographical references.

105. Barclay, Michael J., William G. Christie, Jeffrey H. Harris, Eugene Kandel, and Paul H. Schultz. "The Effects of Market Reform on the Trading Costs and Depths of Nasdaq Stocks." *Journal of Finance* 54 (February 1999): 1-34.

Focuses on relative merits of dealer versus auction markets. Studies implications of SEC reforms that would permit the public to compete directly with Nasdaq dealers by submitting binding limit orders. Study measures impact of new rules on various measures of performance, including trading costs and depths. Study indicates that quoted and effective spreads fell dramatically without affecting adversely market quality. Provides bibliographical references.

106. Bary, Andrew. "The Trader: Ugly Friday caps Nasdaq's Ugliest Week Ever." *Barron's* 17 April 2000, p. MW5+

Reports that major market indexes suffered their steepest single-day point decline Friday, April 14, 2000. The Nasdaq endured sizable losses in each session last week and dropped on Friday, April 14, 355 points. It left the technology benchmark down a record 25.3% for the week. Nasdaq issues sustaining losses of over 40% included CMGI, and Echostar Communications. Reasons for the drop included reaction to government report that consumer prices rose 0.7% and the core rate of inflation was up 0.4%. There were also fears that the Federal Reserve would boost short-term rates. Includes statistical tables.

107. Bessembinder, H. "The Degree of Price Regulation and Equity Trading Costs." *Journal of Financial Economics* 45 (July 1997): 9-34.

Investigates relations between trade execution costs and price-rounding practices for NYSE and Nasdaq listed firms. Focuses on conducting empirical tests regarding collusion hypothesis as set forth in 1994 Christie-Schultz study. Reviews alternative explanations for avoidance of odd-eighth quotes. Examines three measures of trading costs: bid-ask spreads, effective bid-ask spreads, and realized bid-ask spreads. Draws on a sample of 300 Nasdaq listed firms and 300 size-matched NYSE listed firms. Results of study indicate that higher execution costs are associated with rounding of quotations and trade prices. Investigates relations between price rounding and information content of trades. Implies that larger trade execution costs associated with rounded prices can be justified by variation in observable market making costs for NYSE issues but cannot be similarly justified for Nasdaq issues. Results of analyses fail to refute collusion hypothesis and support findings of the SEC in its 1996 study. States that an interesting area for further research should come from impact of reforms on the structure of NASD and execution costs on the Nasdaq. Provides bibliographical references.

108. Blumenthal, Robin Goldwyn. "Closing the Book on Research that Actually made a difference." *Barron's* 18 January 1999, p. 12.

Describes the major impact of the Christie-Schultz 1994 study. As a result of lawsuits and investigations triggered by the study, Nasdaq is spending $100 million on improved surveillance, and a record $1.03 billion settlement of a class action investor lawsuits with dealers alleged to have overcharged them. Additionally, there are $26.3 million in SEC fines against 28 securities firms. Reports reactions of Christie and Schultz who were vindicated through the outcomes of the lawsuits and investigations.

109. Cavanaugh, Katherine. "Nasdaq Chief Reveals his Global Game Plan." *Wall Street and Technology* 17 (December 1999): 14.

Details plans for global expansion of Nasdaq. Frank Zarb, Chair of NASD, reported that, in the future, Nasdaq's Asian, European, and Asian markets will be electronically linked to each other.

110. Chan, Louis K.C. and J. Lakonishok. "Institutional Equity Trading Costs: NYSE versus Nasdaq." *Journal of Finance* 52 (June 1997): 713-735.

Compares execution costs (market impact plus commission on the NYSE and Nasdaq for institutional investors). Controlling the firm size, trade size, and money management firm's identity, costs are lower on Nasdaq for trades in comparatively smaller firms, and costs for trading the larger stocks are lower on Nasdaq. Cost differences estimated from a regression model are sensitive to choice of time period. Studies and compares trading procedures on NYSE and Nasdaq. Data records transactions made by each of 33 large investment management firms each day from January 1989 to December 1991. Provides statistical tables and bibliographical references.

111. Christie, William G. and Paul H. Schultz. "Dealer Markets under Stress: The Performance of Nasdaq Market Makers During the November 15, 1991 Market Break." *Journal of Financial Services Management* 13 (Issue 3):205-229.

Examines effects of November 15, 1991 market break, the first major correction in the Post 1987 Crash era. Examines ramifications of the 1987 Crash on Nasdaq. Nasdaq received strong criticism for its performance during the Crash; the liquidity of the Nasdaq Market was severely undermined. As a result, the NASD implemented regulatory changes designed to ensure the integrity of the market during periods of market stress. This study reveals that unlike October 1987, the market did not deteriorate appreciably during the episode on November 15, 1991. Article based on paper presented at the April 1997 Conference, "Ten Years Since the Crash" at the Financial Markets Research Center at the Vanderbilt University, Owen Graduate School of Management. Includes bibliographic references.

112. Christie, William G. "Evening the Odds: Reform of the Nasdaq Stock Market." *Contemporary Finance Digest: An Overview of Recent Finance Literature* 2 (Summer 1998): 5-27.

Describes events that led to reforms of the Nasdaq beginning with the release to the press of the Christie-Schultz findings and conclusions of the Christie-Schultz study. Summarizes main findings of the Christie-Schultz paper and surveys recent research that provide alternative explanations (other than collusion) for absence of odd-eighth quotes. Reviews the series of lawsuits and investigations by SEC and U.S. Department of Justice that followed release of the Christie-Schultz study. Provides example of a taped telephone conversation between market makers discussing the release of the Christie-Schultz study. Concludes that the future is brighter for Nasdaq and NASD because of these reforms. Provides bibliographical references and a glossary of key terms.

113. Christie William G. "An Expensive Beer for the N.A.S.D." *New York Times* 25 August 1996, p. 12.

Christie and Schultz were doctoral students together at the University of Chicago. Christie recalls the time he and Schultz met for a beer at the Western Finance Association meetings in 1993. It was during this meeting that they decided to study prices that individual market makers quote for active Nasdaq stocks. This led to preparation of the 1994 study that found that for a majority of active Nasdaq stocks, market makers avoid odd-eighth quotes. Avoidance of odd-eighth quotes increased the spread or market makers' profit margin to at least $.25 cents a share. Describes news release in 1994 of study results and the high interest in the story. Describes initial reaction of NASD as not recognizing these problems or ignoring them rather than initiating an independent investigation of issues raised in the study. Describes litigation brought by investors and market professionals against the market making firms. Reports settlement of NASD with the SEC; the SEC settlement calls for NASD to spend $100 million over the next five years, "to better police its market." Christie states lessons learned from their study and its ramifications. Maintains that NASD and SEC must remain vigilant. Adds that NASD has been reorganized with securities laws enforcement now under jurisdiction of NASD Regulation, Inc., led by Mary L. Schapiro.

114. Christie, William G. and Paul H. Schultz. "The Initiation and
     Withdrawal of Odd-Eighth Quotes Among Nasdaq Stocks: An
     Empirical Analysis." *Journal of Financial Economics* 52 (June
     1999): 409-442.

Describes ramifications of the 1994 article by Christie and
Schultz--which led to the establishment of the National Association of
Securities Dealers Regulation (NASDR) and special studies by the SEC
and the U.S. Department of Justice. Uses sample of 250 of the largest
Nasdaq stocks from January 1990 to March 1994. Studies Nasdaq
stocks whose market makers initiate (withdraw) odd-eighth quotes.
States that government reports and special studies do not address
question of why some stocks are quoted only in even-eighths and others
are not. Seeks to find factors which induce market makers to initiate
(withdraw) routine use of odd-eighth quotes and if these factors are
consistent with market making costs. Reviews literature of related
studies. Provides bibliographical references.

115. "Collusion in the Stockmarket." *Economist* 346 (January 17,
     1998): 71+

Reviews Christie-Schultz 1994 study and its influence on Nasdaq
reforms. Reviews recent papers and articles that study effects of Nasdaq
reforms.

116. Demsetz, H. "Limit Orders and the Alleged Nasdaq Collusion."
     Journal of Financial Economics 45 (July 1997): 91-96.

Argues that evidence presented in prior studies alleging
collusion, exaggerates possibility of collusion and, if collusion exists,
that it overestimates degree to which it affects spreads. To support
argument, studies the way NYSE and Nasdaq handle limit orders.
Procedural difference in limit orders indicates that measured spreads
come from different sources; on the Nasdaq, from market makers and
on the NYSE, from investor limit orders. States that absence of
transaction cost floor for spreads set on NYSE by investor limit orders
is an important consideration regarding evidence used for belief that
Nasdaq market makers collude. Reports that excess of Nasdaq spreads

over NYSE spreads can be explained, at least in part, by institutional factors not involving collusion. Provides bibliographical references.

117. Dutta, Prajit K. and Ananth Madhavan. "Competition and Collusion in Dealer Markets." *Journal of Finance* 52 (March 1997): 245-276.

Develops game-theoretic model to analyze market makers' intertemporal pricing strategies. Reviews the previous literature, including the 1994 Christie-Schultz study. Objectives of this empirical study are: 1) to analyze whether market makers who compete on price can sustain spreads above competitive levels, even if market makers do not explicitly cooperate to fix prices; 2) to examine the relationship between institutional arrangement specific to Nasdaq and dealer pricing behavior; and 3) to discuss role of public policy in facilitating price competition among dealers. Demonstrates conditions under which market makers who act noncooperatively may set spreads above competitive levels; this behavior is termed implicit collusion. Explicit collusion is where dealers cooperate to fix prices. Distinction between implicit and explicit collusion is important because the two types of behavior have different antitrust implications and require different burdens of proof. Study states that regulators investigating dealer pricing behavior should recognize that excess spreads can arise without explicit price fixing agreements among dealers. Study shows that collusion is more difficult to maintain where volume is heavily concentrated among a few dealers. Analysis suggests, from policy viewpoint, efforts to enhance competition should be focused on restrictions on access to order flow. Provides bibliographical references and mathematical formulas.

118. Eisenbeis, Robert A. "Regulation: Roundtable Looks at the NASDAQ Controversy." *Journal of Retail Banking Services* 17 (Autumn 1995): 63-65.

Summarizes landmark Christie-Schultz study and its consequences, including Justice Department investigation and class action suits. The Financial Economists Roundtable (FER) examined claims and evidence on NASDAQ pricing and alleged collusion at the

FER July 1995 meeting. FER maintained that observing wider spreads was not sufficient for price fixing suit to sustain findings of implicit collusion. FER noted that other structural and behavioral aspects of the market need to be examined in conjunction with comparing spreads. NASDAQ trading rules may also be a contributing factor to the wider spreads. FER calls for more analysis of behavior and performance of NASDAQ.

119. "Finance and Economics: Marry in Haste." *The Economist* 346 (March 21, 1998): 88-91.

Reports announcement of Nasdaq's and Amex's plan to merge. Discusses various class action suits causing revamping of Nasdaq's market trading practices and regulations. Describes possible problems involved in the merger. States that biggest problem could be the "mob of floor traders" which Amex will bring with it.

120. Furbush, Dean, Paul Godek, Margaret Guerin-Calvert, and Bruce Snapp. *Nasdaq Market Structure and the Christie and Schultz Collusion Hypothesis.* Washington, D.C.: Economists, Inc., June 21, 1995. 28 pages.

Examines implications of two academic articles, both "triggering intense scrutiny of the Nasdaq Stock Market, Inc." These articles are: Christie, William G. and Paul H. Schultz. "Why do Nasdaq Market Makers avoid Odd-Eighth Quotes?," *Journal of Finance*, December 1994, pages 1813-1840 and Christie, William G. J.H. Harris, and Paul H. Schultz. "Why Did Nasdaq Market Makers Stop Avoiding Odd-Eighth Quotes?," *Journal of Finance*, December 1994, 1841-1860. Examines authors' conclusion that Nasdaq market makers "collusively avoid odd eighth-quotes." Studies Nasdaq market structure and market conditions "to assess whether these factors are consistent with successful collusion." Paper refutes hypothesis that collusion exists on Nasdaq. Includes bibliographical references.

121. Furbush, Dean and Jeffrey W. Smith. *Quoting Behavior on Nasdaq: The Effects of Clustering on Relative Spreads.* NASD

Working Paper 96-01. Washington, D.C.: NASD, 1996. 1 vol. (various paging).

Empirical study of Nasdaq quoting behavior and finds that quote clustering occurs "across a spectrum far broader than the even eighth and odd eighth dichotomy presented by Christie and Schultz." Contains bibliographical references and statistical tables.

122. "Getting a Fair Shake for Stock Purchasers: Co-author of Nasdaq Study Suggests Changes." *Washington Post* 21 July 1996, p. H05

Transcript of Washington Post staff writer, Brett D. Fromson's interview with William G. Christie, co-author, with Paul H. Schultz of the 1994 research paper. The Justice Department investigation of Nasdaq had ended last week, with agreement with brokerage firms to impose monitoring procedures. Christie commented on implications for investors of price fixing and the Justice Department's and SEC's investigations.

123. Godek, Paul E. "Why Nasdaq Market Makers Avoid Odd-Eighth Quotes." *Journal of Financial Economics* 41 (1996): 465-474.

Focuses on role that preference trading plays in determining quoted spreads. Author maintains that his results contradict collusion hypothesis of Christie-Schultz 1994 study. Raises question of preference trading as possibly inducing an excess supply of market maker services or if preference trading is a necessary component of a diffuse market maker system. Contains statistical figures and tables, and bibliographical references. Reviews and analyzes previous academic studies, in addition to the Christie-Schultz Study.

124. *Going Public: The Nasdaq Stock Market* Washington, D.C.: Nasdaq, 1996. 71 pages.

Describes how to take a company public through an Initial Public Offering (IPO). Describes how to choose an investment banker, a law firm, and an accounting firm. Reviews how to develop the prospectus and the role of the SEC. Discusses advantages of Nasdaq as the market of choice. Compares listing requirements of Nasdaq, Amex, and NYSE.

125. Grossman, Sanford J., Merton H. Miller, Kenneth R. Cone, Daniel R. Fischel, and David J. Ross. "Clustering and Competition in Dealer Markets." *Journal of Law and Economics* 40 (April 1997): 23-60.

Earlier version of this article was prepared at the time the authors were retained as paid consultants to NASD, during time of Justice Department investigation. Refutes allegations of conclusions because of greater clustering of stock quotations on even-eighth on Nasdaq than on NYSE or Amex. Maintains prevalence of clustering in other markets is fundamentally inconsistent with collusion hypothesis. Authors provide competitive theory of clustering. Authors find that when all data are examined, there is no support of claims that implicit pricing agreement collapsed when collusion hypothesis was reported in newspapers in May 1994. Includes statistical tables and bibliographical references.

126. Harris, J. and Paul H. Schultz. "The Importance of Firm Quotes and Rapid Executions: Evidence from the January 1994 SOES Rules Changes." *Journal of Financial Economics* 45 (July 1997): 135-165.

Examines trading in twenty largest Nasdaq stocks at the time of a rule change that reduced largest Small Execution Order Execution System (SOES) trades from 1000 to 500 shares. Studied were over 1.75 million trades in twenty largest Nasdaq stocks from November 1, 1993 through March 31, 1994. Demonstrates that SOES trades contain information regarding short-term price movements and SOES trading declined dramatically with rule change. Reports that quoted and effective spreads were unaffected by rule change. Studies history and structure of SOES. After 1987 market crash, participation in SOES was made mandatory for all Nasdaq dealers. The change in SOES regulation on January 31, 1994 was aimed specifically at SOES bandits. Provides bibliographical references and statistical tables.

127. Henry, David. "Nasdaq, Big Board in Pitching Duel." *USA Today* 12 August 1997, p. B3.

Reports that the battle for listings is escalating between NYSE and Nasdaq. Nasdaq opened "MarketSite" which offered stock issuers and broadcasters a backdrop of 100 video displays. NYSE is discussing changes to Rule 500. Reports that Al Berkeley, President of Nasdaq stated that there will be a number of companies on both sides (Nasdaq and NYSE) switching back and forth. Berkeley maintains that Nasdaq, in the long term, will attract and hold big companies. Article states that reforms were made on Nasdaq during the past year.

128. Homan, Anthony C. *Does Market Fragmentation Matter? A Case Study of Nasdaq Firms that Switched Listings to the NYSE: A Dissertation Submitted in Partial Fulfillment of the Requirements for the Degree of Doctor of Philosophy, George Mason University.* Fairfax, Virginia: George Mason University, 1995. 172 leaves

Studied firms that switched listings from Nasdaq to the NYSE and investigated if there were any significant differences in several indicators of efficiency, volatility, returns, and trading volume between the different types of market structures. Examined firms that switched from Nasdaq to NYSE from January 1, 1993 to September 30, 1993. Found no significant differences in several indicators of efficiency including price discovery, how well the underlying market explained return, response to shocks to volatility and trading volume, information flow to investors, and the independence of volatility and subsequent returns. Found no significant differences in returns, volatility, and trading volume. Study indicated that firms more likely to do well in a switch have relatively lower risk adjusted returns, lower liquidity, and more noise trades. Firms with higher levels of noise trading on Nasdaq may experience increases in risk adjusted returns and liquidity. Reviews history and operation of Nasdaq. Provides bibliographical references.

129. Horowitz, Jed. "Amex-Nasdaq: Big Questions after the Hugs."
     Investment Dealers Digest 23 March 1998, p. 5-6.

Reports announcement of Nasdaq-Amex merger. Reports Frank
Zarb's announcement that there is a "long way to go" in completion of
the merger. Describes implications of merger including question of how
Amex's listed and Nasdaq's over the counter markets will interact.

130. Huang, R. and Hans R. Stoll. "Dealer Versus Auction Markets:
     A Paired Comparison of Execution Costs on Nasdaq and the
     NYSE." *Journal of Financial Economics* 41 (1996): 313-357.

Study finds that execution costs as measured by the quoted
spread, the effective spread, the realized spread, the Roll implied
spread, and the post-trade variability are twice as large for a sample of
NASDAQ stocks as they are for a matched sample of NYSE stocks.
Partial explanations for the difference are provided by differences in
treatment of limit orders and commissions in the two markets.
Concludes that important explanations are the internalization and
preferencing of order flow and the presence of alternative interdealer
trading systems, factors that limit dealers' incentives to narrow spreads
on NASDAQ. Reviews previous studies providing theoretical
comparisons of dealer and auction markets. Provides bibliographical
references.

131. Jickling, Mark. *Nasdaq: Investigations and Reform.* Major studies
     and issue briefs of the Congressional Research   Service.
     Supplement; 1996, 96-214-E. Washington, D.C.: Congressional
     Research Service, Library of Congress, 1996.

Describes investigations by Department of Justice and SEC alleging
price fixing on Nasdaq. Results of investigations include NASD's
splitting itself in two, with the regulatory operation and Nasdaq market
now separate entities. Includes a brief history of Nasdaq and
bibliographical references.

132. Kandel, Eugene and Leslie. Marx. "Nasdaq Market Structure and Spread Patterns." *Journal of Financial Economics* 45 (July 1997): 61-89.

Constructs a model reflecting distinguishing characteristics of the Nasdaq market. Model implies that competition among market makers will not necessarily drive down spreads to level of marginal cost. Provides explanation for odd eighth quote avoidance as described in 1994 Christie-Schultz Study. Demonstrates that market makers can use odd-eighth avoidance as coordination device to increase spreads. Provides bibliographical references and statistical charts and tables.

133. Kandel, Eugene and Leslie Marx. "Odd-Eighth Avoidance as a Defense against SOES Bandits." *Journal of Financial Economics* 51 (January 1999): 85-102.

Studies and analyzes behavior of Nasdaq momentum traders also called SOES bandits. Shows profitability of SOES bandits decreases in bid ask spread, but increases in effective tick size. Discusses plausibility of odd-eighths avoidance by Nasdaq market makers as a defense against SOES bandits. Uses theoretical models to study effects of SOES bandit activity. Reviews origin and organization of Nasdaq's Small Order Execution System (SOES).

134. Kharouf, Jim. "Stock Exchange Merger Woes." *Futures* 17 (May 1998): 14-16.

Announces approval of merger in March 1998 of directors of Nasdaq and Amex. Reports some opposition to the merger by some absentee seat owners who have created a business by leasing and reselling seats. Some absentee seat owners are concerned about the merger weakening their seat values.

135. Kleidon, Allan W. and Robert D. Willig. *Why Do Christie and Schultz Infer Collusion from Their Data?* Menlo Park, CA: Cornerstone Research. 1 vol. (various paging).

Paper poses central question: "Is it reasonable to infer the existence of collusion from the evidence presented by Christie, Harris, and Schultz" in two 1994 studies? Kleidon and Willig find answer to be no. Examines structure of Nasdaq from perspective of industrial organization. Examines how transaction services are priced and documents the differences between Nasdaq and NYSE that can account for differences in quoted spreads. Studies Christie and Schultz's sample from NYSE/AMEX and Nasdaq in relation to use of odd-eighth quotes. Finds that there are many stocks on NYSE and AMEX whose bid and asked quotes are never or seldom expressed in odd-eighths. Maintains Christie and Schultz studies downplay importance of economic variables. Examines changes in spreads in May 1994 for several Nasdaq stocks studied by Christie and Schultz and refutes their hypothesis that spreads declined because of collapse of a conspiracy among market makers. Provides bibliographical references and statistical tables and figures.

136. Klock, Mark and D. Timothy McCormick. *The Impact of Market Maker Competition on Nasdaq Spreads*. NASD Working Paper 98-04. Washington, D.C.: NASD, 1998. 23 pages.

Analyzes monthly information on the number of market makers for 5,288 Nasdaq securities over an eight year period to investigate the impact of competition on spreads. Includes tables and bibliographical references.

137. Krantz, Michael. "The Day the World Ended." *Time* 155 (April 17, 2000): 42.

Reports losses in the Nasdaq Market the previous week, focusing on the dot.com companies which were hit hard and that, for dot.coms, the "party, if not quite over, is definitely winding down."

138. LaPlante, M. and C. Muscarella. "Do Institutions Receive Comparable Execution in the NYSE and Nasdaq Markets? A Transaction Study of Block Trades." *Journal of Financial Economics* 45 (July 1997): 97-134.

Analyzes three issues related to trading structure differences between NYSE and Nasdaq: 1. frequencies of sizes and types of block trades found on Nasdaq and NYSE; 2. immediate price effects of block transactions; and 3. temporary and permanent price effects of blocks. Finds evidence that NYSE system provides greater liquidity for block transactions. Reviews results of earlier studies. Provides statistical tables and bibliographical references.

139. Lohse, Deborah. "Nasdaq Creates Unit to Study Accuracy of its Listed Firms' Financial Claims." *Wall Street Journal* 3 June 1997, p. C24.

Announces that Nasdaq has created a new unit to investigate questionable claims by its listed companies. Nasdaq's "Listing Investigations Unit" is expected to by headed by Gary Sundick, who is currently associate director of the SEC's enforcement division. Unit's goal is to spot companies, especially those on Nasdaq's Small Cap Market, that have falsified or inflated assets, revenue, or other qualifications to be listed on Nasdaq.

140. Lohse, Deborah, Scot J. Paltrow, and Patrick McGeehan. "Nasdaq Dealers Weigh $900 Million Settlement." *Wall Street Journal* 19 December 1997, p. C1+

Reports that over two dozen Nasdaq dealers are in talks to reach a $900 million settlement in a lawsuit with investors in a class-action lawsuit with investors alleging that firms rigged prices over the past few years on the Nasdaq. The possible settlement would bring total settlements agreed to by Wall Street firms to $1 billion. This settlement is from a lawsuit filed in the U.S. District Court in Manhattan in 1994 against 37 firms including Merrill Lynch & Co., Goldman Sachs & Co., and Bear Stearns Companies.

141. Lohse, Deborah. "Payout from Nasdaq-Dealer Settlement Won't Reach Investors Anytime Soon." *Wall Street Journal* 26 December 1997, p. C10+

Reports that thirty firms reached a $910 million dollar settlement with investors who brought a 1994 class action lawsuit filed in the District Court in Manhattan. Reports previous settlements including a Justice Department complaint. States that under terms of the agreement, investors will not receive any of the agreed-upon restitution until at least mid-1999. Delay, according to lawyers who negotiated the payouts, is due to the fact that it will take at least one year to round up all the investors who might have a valid claim.

142. Lux, Hal. "Justice Department requests Instinet documents on Nasdaq." *Investment Dealers Digest* 61 (February 6, 1995): 6.

Reports Justice Department's request that Instinet Corp., the leading off-exchange Corp. turn over documents and information related to the antitrust probe of Nasdaq. Since the start of the investigation in 1994, The Justice Department has been requesting a large number of trading records and documents.

143. Lux, Hal. "Nasdaq Market Makers seek Dismissal of Collusion Suits." *Investment Dealers Digest.* 61 (May 1, 1995): 5.

Reports the previous week's district court hearing regarding consolidated lawsuit alleging collusion in Nasdaq marketplace. Nasdaq market makers requested Judge Robert Sweet to dismiss the case. The judge did not immediately respond to this request. Reports comments of William Christie concerning the case.

144. Lux, Hal. "Nasdaq retains Nobel laureate for Anti-trust Case Defense." *Investment Dealers Digest* 61 (March 13, 1995): 3.

Reports hiring by Nasdaq of Merton Miller, a Nobel laureate in economics at the University of Chicago. Miller has been assigned to critique the Schultz-Christie 1994 study that triggered the investigations and lawsuits. Miller had written a major study of the October 1987 Stock Market Crash for the Chicago Mercantile Exchange. Miller also had served as Ph.D. advisor to both William Christie of Vanderbilt University and Paul Schultz of Ohio State University. Also hired by

Nasdaq is Sanford Grossman, a professor at the University of Pennsylvania. Grossman has been assigned to review criticism against Nasdaq.

145. Lux, Hal. "Nasdaq's Original Critics Prepare a New Critique." *Investment Dealers' Digest.* 62 (January 29, 1996): 3.

Reports the completion of a new study on Nasdaq trading by William Christie and Paul Schultz. The study raises new questions regarding Nasdaq market makers. Christie and Schultz report extreme shifts in the way Nasdaq market makers quote stocks; the market makers abruptly start and stop using odd-eighth quotes. Reports effects of the original 1994 Christie-Schultz study on the Nasdaq market.

146. McLean, Bethany. "Did Nasdaq Reforms Backfire?" *Fortune* 139 (March 1, 1999): 250-251.

Discusses problems with small-cap stocks (market capitalization under $1 billion). They have underperformed for the past five years and trade at historical lows. Some traders, strategists, and portfolio managers blame Nasdaq reforms. Nasdaq reforms came as a result of studies by the SEC and the Department of Justice and were designed to help individual investors by decreasing trading costs.

147. Morgenson, Gretchen. "Surrender!" *Forbes* 161 (April 6, 1998): 119-120.

Reports March 1998 announcement of Nasdaq-American Stock Exchange merger. Reports of changes in Nasdaq rules as result of Justice Department investigation accusing Nasdaq of collusion which would keep spreads high. Discusses implications of merger for both Nasdaq and Amex.

148. *The NASD Select Committee on Structure and Governance Report.* Hon. Warren B. Rudman, Chair; Jean W. Gleason, Peter S. Lynch, et al. New York: Paul, Weiss, Rifkind, Wharton &

Garrison, 1995. 1 volume (various paging)

Best known as "Rudman Report," this is a landmark study of NASD and Nasdaq and led to major reforms. Report prepared as a result of public criticism of NASD, its oversight of member firms, and its stewardship of Nasdaq. Describes structure, history, and governance of NASD. Reports NASD regulation as "flawed and uneven." Reports Justice Department investigation which came in response to Christie and Schultz academic study asserting that market makers collude in setting prices on the Nasdaq market. NASD subsequently asked former U.S. Senator Warren Rudman to lead review of NASD governance and oversight. Rudman led study of NASD governance and structure and its oversight of the Nasdaq market, without duplicating pending SEC and Justice Department investigations. The study found that fundamental change was required concerning NASD's relationship with Nasdaq. The study recommended restructuring the Nasdaq subsidiary as a relatively autonomous entity, not divorced from NASD, but with "as much autonomy over the Nasdaq and other OTC markets, as the law will allow. The study found that the NASD's structure has failed to keep pace with the expansion and growth of the Nasdaq.

149. "Nasdaq and AMEX: Separate but Equal." *Wall Street and Technology* 5 (May 1998): 12.

Reports at the time of announcement of merger, Nasdaq and Amex planned to keep their two trading systems separate but equal. Reports that this did not work out. According to Frank Zarb, chairman and CEO of NASD, the NASD "will jointly develop a fully automated electronic limit order facility for equities."

150. "Nasdaq Hires Nobel Laureate to Help Fend Off Allegations." *Los Angeles Times* 14 March 1995, p. D2

Announces hiring of Nobel Prize winner Merton Miller by Nasdaq, to fight charges of collusion. Miller will review 1994 Christie-Schultz Study.

151. Nassar, David S. *How to Get Started in Electronic Day Trading: Everything You Need to Know to Play Wall Street's Hottest Game.* New York: McGraw-Hill, 1999. 233 pages.

Chapter 5 is "Thinking Like and Trading with the NASDAQ market makers. Includes some of the history and organization of NASDAQ and focuses on its Level II Trading Screen.

152. Norton, Leslie P. "Why the Nasdaq Market Matters." *Far Eastern Economic Review* 163 (April 13, 2000): 37.

Reports that if Nasdaq market turns lower, Asian investors should start worrying. Nasdaq is important to Asian investors since it is a major subcontractor for hi-tech outfits and a major consumer-electronics exporter.

153. "The Odd Couple Wins." *Economist* 338 (January 13, 1996): 70.

Describes ramifications of the Christie-Schultz 1994 study, which was named the *Journal of Finance*'s "Paper of the Year" at the American Finance Association's annual meetings on January 6, 1996.

154. Orenstein, David. "NASD Considers Trading Halts." *Computerworld* 33 (February 22, 1999): 93.

Reports that NASD is considering increasing its authority to halt trading immediately when significant news about a company is reported or when a stock is trading with extraordinary volatility. Other measures taken by NASD include stepping up the monitoring of day trading.

155. Paltrow, Scot J. "Anger over Stock Manipulation Allegation." *Los Angeles Times* 19 July 1996, p. D2.

Describes angry reactions from institutional investors and others buying Nasdaq stocks. Reactions came after Justice Department alleged Nasdaq dealers manipulated stock prices.

156. Paltrow, Scot J. "Nasdaq Dealers Reportedly Settle in Federal Probe." *Los Angeles Times* 13 July 1996, p. A1+

Reports that major Nasdaq Stock Market dealers reached a tentative settlement on July 12, 1996 with the Antitrust Division of the U.S. Department of Justice. The investigation had been underway since 1994 and involved major firms including Merrill Lynch, Smith Barney, and Goldman Sachs. The investigation focused on collusion charges among dealer firms to increase spreads on Nasdaq Stocks. A private antitrust class action suit is still pending in federal court in New York.

157. Paltrow, Scot J. "Nasdaq Releases Studies Aiming to Disprove Allegations of Collusion Securities: Two Reports Claim that Competition between Dealers is Strong and that Price Spreads are a Natural Occurrence." *Los Angeles Times* 6 April 1995, p. 1.

Relates results of two Nasdaq commissioned studies that aim to disprove allegations of collusion to fix prices of Nasdaq stocks. The studies are to be unveiled at a conference on financial markets reform at the Owen Graduate School of Management at Vanderbilt University. One study is by Merton Miller, Nobel Laureate economist at the University of Chicago and Kenneth R. Cone, vice-president of Lexecon, Inc. The second study is by Dean Furbush of Economists, Inc. Both studies aim to refute Christie-Schultz 1994 study.

158. Paltrow, Scot J. "Nasdaq Studies May Prove Academic Wall Street: Legal Experts say Hard Evidence is What will matter in most Collusion Probes." *Los Angeles Times* 7 April 1995, p. 2.

Reports reaction of Nobel Laureate, Merton Miller to Christie-Schultz 1994 study. At a conference at Vanderbilt University, Miller called the study flawed setting off wasteful lawsuits and possible harmful intervention by regulatory officials. Miller maintained that the Nasdaq market "is unquestionably competitive." Paltrow reports that the SEC and the Justice Department are reviewing numerous documents and tapes of telephone conversations between Nasdaq dealers. At the Vanderbilt University conference, Blair Hull, managing partner of Hull

Trading Co. stated that he had experienced pressure from dealers regarding the narrowing of spreads. Dean Furbush, author of a study for Nasdaq, stated that pricing is fully competitive.

159. Paltrow, Scot J. "SEC Chief Lectured Securities Dealers' Board." *Los Angeles Times* 21 November 1995, p. D2.

Relates closed-door meeting where SEC Chairman Arthur Levitt, Jr. sternly lectured the NASD Board about need to reform Nasdaq. Levitt warned that SEC was likely to file disciplinary charges against NASD.

160. Paltrow, Scot J. "SEC Plans Civil Charges in Its Nasdaq Probe." *Los Angeles Times* 7 July 1995, p. A1+

Reports that SEC is expected to file civil charges, as early as September, against the NASD. Charges will stem from findings that the NASD failed to take steps to stop manipulation of stock prices on Nasdaq. Describes reaction by NASD.

161. Paltrow, Scot J. "Taped Conversations Indicate Abuses, SEC Says." *Los Angeles Times* 9 August 1996, p. D12.

A SEC report issued August 8, 1996 made public portions of tape recorded conversations among Nasdaq market makers. The tapes appear to contain evidence that traders conspired to keep profit margins wide, to manipulate basic stock prices, and to violate rule requiring trades be reported within 90 seconds of execution. Dealers' spokespersons deny conversations contain such evidence.

162. Paltrow, Scot J. "U.S. Accuses Nasdaq Dealers of Manipulating Stock Prices." *Los Angeles Times* 18 July 1996, p. D1+

Reports Justice Department allegations that some major dealers in Nasdaq stocks colluded with each other to manipulate stock prices. Dealers involved include Merrill Lynch, Smith Barney, Goldman

Sachs, and Prudential Securities. Attorney General Janet Reno stated that conspiracy among dealers cost individual investors "many millions of dollars." Justice Department findings support Christie-Schultz 1994 academic paper.

163. Petruno, Tom. "NASDAQ Changes Level Playing Field."
     Newsday 19 January 1997, p. F7.

Describes changes in rules involving trading of Nasdaq stocks, to go into effect on January 20, 1997. Changes allow small investors to "determine second-by-second prices for Nasdaq stocks." Prior to this only institutional investors would have this control. Change in ruling took place as result of a Justice Department investigation. The author explains to investors the implications and phases of changes in rulings.

164. Power, William. "Nasdaq Study's Co-author Keeps Clear of
     Aftermath." *Wall Street Journal* 2 August 1995, p. C1 +

Discusses the impact of the Nasdaq investigations and lawsuits on co-author, William Christie of Vanderbilt University. Christie had turned down offers to be a paid consultant in the lawsuits. Christie states that he did not regret using the word "collusion" in the 1994 Christie-Schultz study. Paul Schultz stated that he would use the word "collusion" again since it called attention to Nasdaq and need for reforms.

165. Sales, Robert. "Nasdaq's Technology Triathlon." *Wall Street and
     Technology* 16 (July 1998): 38-42.

Describes NASD's overseeing technology projects involving Nasdaq. The technology projects are related to the pending Nasdaq-Amex merger; the Nasdaq Order Delivery and Execution System (Nodes), and a trading technology partnership with Optimark Technologies. Greg Bailar, the chief information officer of NASD was interviewed for this article. Provides illustrations of Nasdaq's

Manhattan based MarketSite media wall and the recently established
Hardiman Technology Center in Trumbull, Connecticut.

166. Simaan, Yusif, Daniel G. Weaver, and David K. Whitcomb.
Market Maker Quotation Behavior and Pre-Trade Transparency.
Working Paper. New York: Baruch College, 2000. 38 pages.

Examines impact of Nasdaq rule changes on quote price
competition. Focuses on quotation behavior of market makers following
reduction of tick size from eighths to sixteenths on June 2, 1997 and
the direct impact of including electronic communication network (ECN)
quotes in the calculation of inside Nasdaq quotes. Develops model that
predicts that market makers are more likely to quote on all ticks if they
are able to do so anonymously. Finds that following tick size reduction,
Nasdaq market makers again appear to be avoiding odd ticks, but
consistent with prediction of authors' model, trades entering orders on
ECNs appear more likely to use all ticks. Also finds that: 1. ECNs
establish the "inside market" and therefore reduce trading costs for the
public, approximately 19% of the time and 2. Market makers that place
anonymous limit orders on ECNs have higher propensity to actively
narrow spread than they do when quoting in Nasdaq quote montage.
Results indicate, from regulatory perspective, that although some
market reform improved market quality, some major impediments to
quote price competition still exist. Discusses Christie-Schultz 1994
study and investigations by SEC and U.S. Department of Justice.
Reviews literature that offers explanations of Christie-Schultz findings.
Contains bibliographical references, footnotes, and statistical tables.

167. Smith, Anne Kates. "NYSE and Nasdaq: Dollars and Common
Cents." *U.S. News and World Report* 16 June 1997, p. 54.

Reports that NYSE will stop quoting stock quotes in eighth of
a dollar. States that it will use sixteenths at the end of June and switch
to decimals by January 2000. Nasdaq is quoting in sixteenth and is
examining a switch to decimals.

168. Smith, Geoffrey, Mike McNamee and Leah Nathans Spiro. "Day of Reckoning for Day-trading Firms?" *Business Week* 3612 (January 18, 1999): 88+

Reports in growth in day-trading industry since 1988. There are more firms using new software designed to execute split-second trading. Traders sign on with day trading firms which are licensed by NASD and have special software providing information on flow of orders and instant access to Nasdaq stocks. Provides case studies where individuals have experienced significant losses. States that industry regulators are monitoring day-trading firms.

169. Smith, Jeffrey W. *The Effects of Order Handling Rules and 16ths on Nasdaq: A Cross-sectional Analysis.* NASD Working Paper, 98-02. Washington, D.C.: NASD, 1998. 36 pages.

Empirical analysis of the impact of two significant changes on the Nasdaq in 1997: the implementation of the SEC's Order Handling Rules and a reduction in the quotation ticker size for many Nasdaq stocks from 1/8th to 1/16th. Studies impact of changes on spreads, depth, use of Electronic Communications Networks, and market making positions. Study revealed that "many stocks experienced major changes in their trading characteristics, other stocks particularly thinly traded issues, were largely unaffected."

170. Trombly, Maria. "NASD asks SEC to Postpone Stock Decimalization Push." *Computerworld* 34 (March 13, 2000): 6.

Reports that NASD asked the SEC to postpone until 2001 plans to shift securities markets to decimal based pricing. This postponement would help Nasdaq increase system capacity to handle the expected increase in data traffic, with the decimalization.

171. U.S. Department of Justice. Antitrust Division. *U.S. vs. Alex. Brown & Sons, et al. (U.S. versus Nasdaq Market Makers, Competitive Impact Statement.* Washington.D.C., U.S. Dept. of Justice, 1996. 1 vol. (various paging).

The study of Nasdaq market makers was brought about as result of Christie-Schultz 1994 study, suggesting collusion. The U.S. alleges in its Complaint that "defendants and others adhered to and enforced a "quoting convention" that was designed to and did deter price competition among the defendants and other market makers in their trading of Nasdaq stocks with the general public." The Justice Department's investigation began during the Summer 1994 and subsequently reviewed large numbers of pages of documents produced by the defendants and other market participants in response to over 350 Civil Investigative Demands. Also reviewed were approximately 4500 hours of audio tapes of telephone conversations between stock traders employed by defendants and other Nasdaq market makers. Additionally, the Justice Department conducted telephone and in-person interviews of current and former Nasdaq stock traders, Nasdaq investors, and others with knowledge related to the industry. Provides transcripts of selected interviews and tapes of phone conversations. Explains terminology and offers examples of terms used in investigations, including "dealer quotes and the dealer spread" and "inside quotes and the inside spread." U.S. Dept. of Justice investigation confirms systematic avoidance of odd-eighth quotes, collusion, and peer pressure among Nasdaq market makers to maintain conformity in dealer spreads. Also refers to peer pressure in article, "Fun and Games on Nasdaq," published in *Forbes*, August 1993.

172. U.S. Securities and Exchange Commission. *Report Pursuant to Section 21(a) of the Securities Exchange Act of 1934 Regarding the NASD and the Nasdaq Market.* Washington, D.C.: U.S. Securities and Exchange Commission, August 8, 1996. 1 vol. (various paging).

Investigation of the NASD and market making activities in the Nasdaq Stock Market. According to the introduction, the SEC "believes that significant changes to the NASD and the NASDAQ market are warranted." Finds that NASD violated SEC 19 (g) of the Exchange Act by failing adequately to comply with certain NASD rules and without reasonable justification or excuse to enforce compliance with Exchange Act and rules. The primary focus is whether NASD adequately carried out its obligation under the Exchange Act to oversee the Nasdaq market and conduct of its members. Study came about as a result of 1994

Christie-Schultz academic paper which described implicit collusion among Nasdaq market makers. SEC report maintains that NASD failed to conduct appropriate inquiry into anticompetitive pricing practices among Nasdaq market makers. Recommends that the NASD must renew its commitment to the interest of the public and public investors in the Nasdaq. Describes key events and reports in the history of NASD and Nasdaq and describes work of NASD Select Committee on Structure and Governance, Chaired by former U.S. Senator Warren Rudman and the subsequent report. Describes remedial measures implemented by NASD: the creation of two subsidiaries 1. NASD Regulation (NASDR), responsible for regulatory matters and 2. Nasdaq Stock Market, Inc. whose primary responsibility is to run Nasdaq. Provides Appendices that elaborate on certain issues identified, including statistical tables and transcripts of tapes of Nasdaq market makers.

173. Viswanathan, K.G., George Papaioannou, and Steven Krull. "Testing for Liquidity Gains in the Market Reaction to Nasdaq National Market System Phase-ins." *Quarterly Journal of Business and Economics* 36 (Summer 1997): 49-61

Examines whether market reaction to stock movements from regular Nasdaq to Nasdaq National Market System is explained by changes in liquidity costs and whether the relationship between pre-NMS spreads and market reaction to NMS transfers is consistent with realized liquidity cost changes. Studies whether number of market makers affects predictive power of pre-NMS spreads as price reaction to NMS phase-ins. Studies sample of 672 stocks phased in from 1983-1991. Tests confirm that market reaction to NMS transfers is directly related to reductions in spreads. Findings also indicate that price reaction is positively related to potential for liquidity gains as measured by level of pre-NMS bid-ask spreads. The pre-NMS number of market makers does not impact adversely the pre-NMS spread and market reaction relationship. Reviews findings of previous studies and includes statistical tables and bibliographical references.

174. *The Wall Street Journal Guide to Who's Who and What's What on Wall Street.* By the Editors of the *Wall Street Journal.* New

York: Ballantine Books, 1998. 530 pages.

Includes a chapter, "The Nasdaq Stock Market in the Throes of Change" which reports changes imposed on NASD and Nasdaq as result of investigations by the SEC and the Justice Department. Provide reprints of key articles published in the *Wall Street Journal* at the time of the investigations and special studies. Reviews ramifications of the 1994 Christie-Schultz Study. Contains biographical profiles of key people in NASD and Nasdaq, including Frank Zarb, Chairman, President, and Chief Executive Officer of NASD; Richard G. Ketchum, Executive Vice-President and Chief Operating Officer, NASD; Dean Furbush, Chief Economist of NASD; Mary Schapiro, President of NASDR; and Alfred R. Berkeley III, President of Nasdaq.

175. Wansley, James W., Philip R. Daves, and David B. Stewart. *Volume and Liquidity Differences between the Exchanges and Nasdaq.* Working paper. Knoxville, Tennessee: University of Tennessee, Department of Finance, January 1997. 30 pages.

Develops model that allows adjustment of reported Nasdaq volume so that it is comparable with exchange reported volume through examining the cross-sectional determinants of the change in reported volume when firms switch from OTC trading to exchange listing. Sample studied is from firms that stopped trading on Nasdaq and immediately listed on NYSE or Amex from May 1983 to June 1993. Finds that volume after listing on NYSE or Amex averages 58% of the volume reported by Nasdaq prior to listing. Results suggest that liquidity is enhanced when firms move from Nasdaq to NYSE and reduced when firms move from Nasdaq to Amex. Includes statistical tables and bibliographical references.

176. Warner, Melanie. "Nasdaq's Brand-New, 55-Foot Wall O'Tech: Who's it For?" *Fortune* 135 (May 26, 1997): 36-37.

Reports unveiling of MarketSite, a giant 55-foot wall of 100 video monitors with displays ranging from stock price charts to CNN reporters. Frank Zarb states that MarketSite is an information resource for individual investors some of whom do not have access to a

Bloomberg machine. Others at Nasdaq state that MarketSite is for issuing companies and Wall Street firms; MarketSite would be used for analysts' conferences.

177. Warner, Melanie. "The Troublemakers who cause Nasdaq Volatility." *Fortune* 134 (December 23, 1996): 30-31.

Discusses effects of SOES bandits on Nasdaq market. SOES bandits are traders of Nasdaq stock that get their name from the Small Order Execution System (SOES) and work with the SOES system. SOES bandits buy and sell on lots that never exceed 1,000 shares. The rapid buying and selling by SOES bandits is blamed for Nasdaq market volatility.

178. Wipperfurth, Heike. "Staffers Anxiety Mounts as NASD/Amex Merger Looms."*Investment Dealers Digest* 14 September 1998, p. 12.

Reports that staff members of both stock markets are anxious about merger. Staffers report little information from their respective managements concerning organizational implications of merger. However, Michael Jones, NASD's chief administrative officer reports that an integration team has been formed; the team represents various divisions at Amex and NASD and led by NASD's deputy chief operating officer and chief financial officer, Salvatore Sodano. The team is working on a plan involving 617 employees at Amex and 3000 employees working for Nasdaq, NASD, and NASDR.

179. Woolley, Suzanne and Paula Dwyer. "Market of the Future? Don't Hold Your Breath." *Business Week* 3571 (March 30, 1998): 36.

Describes positive features of proposed Nasdaq-Amex merger. These include establishing more efficient markets and creating a more formidable rival to the New York Stock Exchange. Discusses drawbacks of merger including problems involved in introducing structural changes at the exchanges. Describes similar problems at

London Stock Exchange and the InterVest Financial Services.

180. Zarb, Frank G. *Testimony of Frank G. Zarb, Chairman and Chief Executive Officer, National Association of Securities Dealers, Inc. before the Senate Committee on Banking, Housing and Urban Affairs on the Future of Securities Markets, February 29, 2000.* Washington, D.C., National Association of Securities Dealers, 2000. 21 pages.

Statement of Frank G. Zarb's vision of the future of the securities markets and the regulatory environment in which they will operate. Addresses whether technological and marketplace changes will continue the preeminence of U.S. markets into the future. Reviews role and organization of NASD. Discusses history and organization of Nasdaq and includes statistical tables regarding its hi-tech market share. Predicts future developments which include: securities will be digital, global and accessible twenty-four hours; stock quotes will be available instantly and executions of trade can be done instantly, at any time; trading floors and paper will, for the most part, be made obsolete by technology and competition; investors will be able to use, not only computers, but cellular phones, pagers, and palm-sized computers to access markets; and investors will be able to obtain stock performance reports via car radios and/or digital televisions. Discusses proposed Super Montage system or Nasdaq Order Display Window. Among its capabilities, Super Montage will display the best bid and best offer in Nasdaq and two price levels away from best bid and offer.

181. Zipser, Andy. "Hey Kids--If You're Looking for Heroes--Here's Two of 'Em." *Barron's* 22 July 1996, p. 10.

Announces that the Justice Department wrapped up their two-year investigation of Nasdaq trading the previous week. Attorney General Janet Reno stated that "millions of dollars had been manipulated" out of pockets of consumers. Evidence reviewed by Justice Department included taped conversations between traders that showed evidence of collusion. Article praises Christie-Schultz and their 1994 study which triggered lawsuits and investigations of Nasdaq market makers.

CHAPTER VIII
STATISTICS SOURCES

The following materials contain statistics concerning the Nasdaq Stock Market, including Dow Jones Averages, Nasdaq indexes, daily prices, volume, etc. Depending on the source, statistics can be presented on a daily, weekly, or monthly basis and some materials offer historical data. Sources listed are in paper, CD-ROM, and online formats. Major web sites, including Nasdaq's own site and others such as Motley Fool and Bloomberg, are listed here with their URLs. These sites, for the most part, offer free news reports and stock quotes (mostly on time-delayed basis). Sites offering real-time quotes usually require registration. Check individual web sites for further information.

It should be noted that not all newspapers which include Nasdaq data are presented here. Other major daily newspapers such as the *Washington Post, Los Angeles Times, Newsday,* and the *Boston Globe* feature a financial section with data on securities.

182. *American Statistics Index (ASI): A Comprehensive Guide and Index to Statistical Publications of the U.S. Government.* Bethesda, Maryland: Congressional Information Service Inc., a member of the LEXIS-NEXIS Family, URL: http://www.cispubs.com V. 1, 1974-   Monthly index and abstracts issue, plus annual cumulation of indexes and abstracts. Available in paper and online database formats. Available online through LEXIS-NEXIS's *CIS Statistical Universe.*

Guide and index to statistical publications of the U.S. Government covers periodicals, series, special reports, annuals, etc. Issued in two sections, one for the Index, and the other for Abstracts, with description of the statistical publication. Relevant publications may be retrieved in Government Documents depository libraries or by ordering microfiche copies from the Congressional Information Service.

183. *Barron's: The Dow Jones Business and Financial Weekly.* New York: Dow Jones & Co., Inc. V. 1, 1921-   Weekly. URL:http://www.barrons.com

Contains news stories about companies, investment advice, the economy, and the securities markets. The "Market Week" section features trading on issues during previous week's trading and includes statistics for Nasdaq National Market and Nasdaq Small-Cap Issues.

184. Bentley, Linda Holman and Jennifer J. Kiesl. *Investment Statistics Locator.* Rev. and expanded ed. Phoenix, Arizona: Oryx Press, 1996. 275 pages.

Presents statistics for investment related information including Nasdaq Most Active Issues, Nasdaq 100 Index, Nasdaq Block Transactions, and Nasdaq Industrial Index. Among statistical sources indexed are: *Barron's, Analyst's Handbook, New York Times, Wall Street Journal, Value Line,* and Nasdaq Fact Book.

185. *BigCharts* (http://www.bigcharts.com)

Maintained by *CBSMarketWatch. com.*, provides access to market news, stock quotes, and industry analysis. Also provides historical stock price data and stock charts that allow users to prepare customized charts based on various parameters, including stock prices and indexes, and other data.

186. *Bloomberg.com*(http://www.bloomberg.com/markets/index.html)

Provides statistics and financial news reports. Includes stock market prices for Nasdaq and data on tech stocks and most active stocks. Also features a Fed Watch and news about technology, world politics, and the economy.

187. *Business Week.* New York: Business Week, V. 1- 1929-
    Weekly. Updated daily on its web site, URL: http://www.businessweek.com

Features section, "Business Week Investor, Figures of the Week" containing data for: S & P 500, Dow Jones Industrials, Nasdaq Composite, Best Performing Groups (by industry), Worst Performing Groups (by Industry), interest rates, mutual funds, company performance data, and projections for the week ahead.

188. *CBS MarketWatch* (http://cbs.marketwatch.com)

Provides access to news stories, delayed time quotes, major indexes including Nasdaq, and advice on personal finance.

189. *CNBC.com* (http://cnbc.com)

Features portfolio tracking, stock market statistics, headline and company news, etc.

190. *CNNFn* (http://www.cnnfn.cnn.com)

Contains data on the markets and news releases about companies, CEOs, the economy, world business, and finance. Features market outlook reports and advice on personal finance.

191. *The Center for Research in Security Prices (CRSP).* (http:gsbwww.uchicago.edu/research/crsp/)

Maintained by the Center for Research in Security Prices, a financial research center at the Graduate School of Business at the University of Chicago. Provides comprehensive historical data files on the securities market, including Nasdaq. Scope of coverage includes: daily and month-end stock data, daily and monthly stock and U.S. Treasury Indices, mutual funds, reformatted COMPUSTAT Industrial Company Data with CRSPLink, a link between CRSP stock and COMPUSTAT fundamental data; and daily and monthly U.S. treasurers. CRSP data files are distributed on CD-ROM through subscription and Internet access to all CRSP data is available to academic subscribers through Wharton (http://wrds.upenn.edu) and access to commercial subscribers of the CRSP Stock Data is available through FACTSet (http://www.factset.com).

192. *Compustat PC Plus.* New York: Standard & Poor's. Available on CD-ROM.

Database, with software, available on CD-ROM provides public company information, including income statements, balance sheets, and financial ratios. Also covers economic data including Gross Domestic Product, inflation rate, unemployment rate, and Consumer Price Index. Contains S & P Analysts Consensus Estimates (ACE), a consensus of analysts estimates and stock recommendations. Includes Daily Prices History, a database covering up to five years of daily stock price history. *Compustat PC Plus* allows users to prepare custom reports.

193. *Data Broadcasting Corporation (DBC)* (http://www.dbc.com).

Features fast quote allowing searches for specific stock prices. Also provides quick stock charts, symbol lookup, headline news, major market indexes, volume leaders, and market movers.

194. *Electronic Dividend Service*. New York: Mergent FIS Available
through dial-in or ftp.

   Service provides latest data on over 22,000 dividend-paying
stocks and mutual funds for United States and Canada. Provides data
on: return of capital, payment frequency, stock splits, payment
frequency rate, etc.

195. *FISOnline*. Source: Mergent FIS. URL: http://www.fisonline.com

   Database contains: FIS Company Archives, with descriptions for
over 4,000 companies; FactSheets, including over 1700 summary
company reports for companies traded on NYSE and Nasdaq/Amex;
Real-Time News, featuring the latest company and stock market
information; FIS Institutional Holdings, enables research of the largest
institutional holders for U.S. companies; FIS Insider Trading, supplies
statistics on all share buys and sells by U.S. corporate officers and
directors for the past three and six months; and Earnings Estimates,
provides Wall Street consensus estimates on all companies in the
database followed by at least one Wall Street analyst.

196. *Financial Times (North American edition)* New York: Financial
Times, 1985- Monthly. URL: http://www.ftmarketwatch.com

   International focus, with news stories about world news,
politics, companies, the economy, and finance. Provides statistics for
trading on the Nasdaq Stock Market. Its web site, *FT Market Watch*
provides data on international markets, including Nasdaq, stock quotes,
current news stories, and portfolio tracking.

197. *FOX Market Wire.* (http://www.foxmarketwire.com)

   Current news stories about world events, the economy, politics,
and the markets. Registration at site allows access to real-time stock
quotes.

198. *FreeEdgar* (http://www.freedgar.com)

Searchable site of SEC Edgar filings, providing access to the day's new filings. Special feature is Watchlist, which send e-mail alerts when companies submit new filings to the SEC.

199. *Freerealtime* (http://www.freerealtime.com)

Registration is required for real-time quotes. Contains market summary, including Dow Jones Industrial Average and Nasdaq indexes; analyses of stocks; RADAR, stocks on the move; message board; and latest news.

200. *Guide to Special Issues and Indexes of Periodicals* Edited by Miriam Uhlan and Doris B. Katz. 4th ed. Washington, D.C.: Special Libraries Association, 1994. 223 pages.

Guide to periodicals with special issues that focus on various topics and present statistics. Check index for entry number of periodical title. Each entry contains name, address, frequency, where indexed, list of special issues for the periodical, and month(s) of special issues.

201. *The Handbook of Dividend Achievers.* New York: Mergent FIS. Annual.

Reports dividend records for companies that have raised their annual dividends for at least 10 consecutive calendar years. Three hundred twenty companies have qualified for inclusion. Each company record contains: company overviews, recent developments, stock movement charts, company background, etc.

202. *The Handbook of Nasdaq Stocks.* New York: Mergent FIS. Quarterly

For over 600 companies on Nasdaq, covers: company overviews, recent developments, stock movement charts, price performance statistics, institutional holdings, financial performance indicators, and company background. Also includes rankings of companies with the highest short and long term price score and 25 stocks with highest and lowest P/E ratios.

203. *Historical Market Data Center.* New York: Dow-Jones Interactive

Online database provides pricing history for financial issues, including stocks, bonds, mutual funds, market indexes, and options.

204. *Hoover's Online.* Austin, Texas: Hoovers, Inc. URL: http://www.hoovers.com

Provides public and private company data, industry statistics, business and company news, stock market data, list of IPOs, and career information.

205. *Internet Stock News* (http://www.netstocks.com)

Contains news and statisitcs about Internet stocks and companies. Features message boards, ticker symbol searching, news reports, and stock offerings.

206. *Investorama* (http://www.investorama.com)

Extensive site features stock market and mutual fund statistics, best of the web directory, guide to starting an investment club, investor's glossary, personal finance tools, message boards, and financial news. Some sections require registration.

207. *Investor's Business Daily.* Los Angeles, California: Investor's Business Daily, Inc. 1991- (Formerly: *Investor's Daily*, V. 1, 1984 - V. 8,No. 110, September 13, 1991). Also provides *Investors.com* (http://www.investors.com)

Provides NASDAQ Composite, NASDAQ Tables with IBD SmartSelect Corporate Ratings, and NASDAQ Stocks in the News. NASDAQ Tables provide stock name, stock symbol, closing price, earnings per share, relative price strength, and industry group relative strength. Also provides features on companies, industries, and the economy. Its web site, *Investors.com* features current business and finance news and statistics.

208. *Just Quotes* (http://www.justquotes.com)

Searchable web site provides searching by company name or ticker symbol. For each company, includes time-delayed stock quotes, real-time quotes (registration required), one-month stock chart, analysts' recommendations, discussion boards, and links to other web sites, including SEC filings.

209. *Market Guide, Inc.* (http://www.marketguide.com)

Provides market summary, including indexes for S & P 500 and Nasdaq, stock market quotes, and stock selection advice.

210. *Money.* New York: Time, Inc. V. 1, 1972-   Monthly. URL: http://www.money.com

Features section "By the Numbers," statistical tables of market benchmarks, including market measures (Nasdaq, S & P 500, etc.); best performing stocks, highest-yielding Dow stocks; widely-held stocks; one-year performance rankings.

211. *Morningstar Mutual Funds.* Chicago, Illinois: Morningstar, Inc., 1991- Bi-weekly. URL: http://www.morningstar.com

Contains full-page reports on over 1700 mutual funds, including 160 closed-end funds. Also features star and category rankings; analyst reviews; editorial spotlights on equity, international, and fixed income markets; rookie fund reports; and summary sections, with updated reports twice a month. The Morningstar web site features stock market statistics plus data on mutual fund, including FundQuick Rank; ratings by various categories; Morningstar ratings of funds; discussion board; and recent news about funds. More detailed reports on web site require subscription.

212. *The Motley Fool.* http://www.fool.com

   Contains the day's headlines, personal finance advice, company news, tax information, discussion boards, and stock market data.

213. *Nasdaq Daily Stock Price Record.* New York: Standard & Poor's. Issued four times per year; volumes may be purchased individually, or on an annual basis.

   Provides section on Major Technical Indicators of the Stock Market, including S & P Indexes, Dow Jones Daily Averages, etc. Contains sections on Mutual Funds, Banks and Insurance Stocks, Industrial Stocks. Bid and asked prices are listed for Mutual Funds and volume, high, low, and closing prices are provided for Banks and Insurance Stocks and Industrial Stocks.

214. "Nasdaq 1000." Annual issue of *Equities Magazine*, (in print and its web site is: http://www.equities magazine.com). Published in September issue.

   Features articles about Nasdaq and its companies. Ranks Nasdaq companies by stock market value and by market value. Provides "Nasdaq 1000" alphabetical directory. Data for each company includes: market value, assets, sales, net income, ticker symbol, company location, and earnings per share. Compares company data with previous years statistics. Profiles companies that have improved their rankings in each of Nasdaq's four critical measures: gain in assets, revenue, earnings, and market value. Contains feature on Nasdaq 1000 newcomers.

215. *The Nasdaq Stock Market* (http://www.nasdaq.com)

Provides: quotes for Nasdaq, Amex, NYSE, and the OTC Bulletin Board; major indices including Nasdaq, Dow Jones, Industrial Average, and S & P 500; recent news headlines; Nasdaq listing information; market outlook; recent IPO filings; company news; Nasdaq 100 FlashQuotes; and Global Market news and data. See also Appendix IV, "The NASD/Nasdaq Family of Web Sites."

216. *The Nasdaq Stock Market: One Billion Plus and Fastest Growing* New York: Moody's Investor Service, 1991. 143 pages.

Profiles two groups of Nasdaq companies: those that have a market capitalization of $1 billion or more and those that are among the top 100 fastest growing companies in the United States. Companies are listed in rank at the beginning of each section, then alphabetically arranged. Each company entry provides: ticker symbol, description of business, annual financial data, name and address of company, recent developments, P/E ratio, trading volume, list of officers, capitalization, etc.

217. *NASDAQ Symbol Book.* New York: Francis Emory Fitch, 1991-

Directory of ticker symbols and CUSIP numbers. Section 1 contains NASDAQ securities arranged alphabetically according to corporate titles, by CUSIP and Section 2 contains NASDAQ securities arranged alphabetically according to symbols.

218. *The Nasdaq-Amex Fact Book and Company Directory* (Formerly *The Nasdaq Fact Book and Company Directory*). Washington, D.C.: The Nasdaq-Amex Market Group, Inc. Annual.

Provides data on performance of Nasdaq securities and Amex securities, options, and derivatives. Contains: the Year in Review; statistics about the American Stock Exchange (Amex); the Nasdaq Company Directory, providing names, addresses, phone numbers, and SIC codes; Nasdaq Companies sorted by SIC Codes; and The Nasdaq

Stock Market--Equities. Statistics presented on Nasdaq Stock Market equities include: share and dollar volume, top initial public offerings by offering value, for the year; Nasdaq monthly short interest; Nasdaq National Market (NMS) monthly short index; total non U.S. companies by year; worldwide distribution of non-U.S. companies for the year; the year's equity trading records; annual share and dollar volume; ten highest share and dollar volume days; annual volume for the past ten years; largest weekly increases; and composite index and sub-indices--monthly closing level. Also provides directory of Nasdaq and NASD related web sites and key telephone numbers.

219. National Association of Securities Dealers, Inc. *NASD Annual Report*. Washington, D.C.: NASD. Annual

Features profile and a brief history of NASD, letter from the Chairman; Directory of the NASD Board of Governors; Statistical Highlights for Nasdaq and Amex; NASD financial statements; Directory of office locations and districts; and list of NASD web sites. The *Annual Report* is available in print and on the NASD and Nasdaq web sites.

220. *The New York Times*. New York: the New York Times Company, 1851- Daily URL: http://www.nytimes.com

The Business section of the *Times*, in addition to articles and features, lists trading statistics for Nasdaq National Market and for Nasdaq Small Capitalization Market. The Databank features stocks in the news, Dow Jones Industrial Average, S & P Index of 500 Stocks, the Nasdaq 100, and the Nasdaq Index.

221. *Online Investor's Sourcebook*. Oak Brook, Illinois: Online Investor Annual issue.

Guide to investing on the web focuses on presenting over 500 reviews of investing and personal finance web sites organized by category. Features "Best Sites of the Year," "Blue-Chip Picks," and "Best New Sites." Categories include: online brokers, global investing,

Wall Street research, market data, economic analysis, options and futures, personal finance, research, stock picks, tax planning, megasites, mutual funds, newsletters, government documents, IPOs, market timing, and news. Describes sites that are: free, require registration, and fee-based.

222. *Primark Global Access.* New York: Thomson Financial URL: http://www primark.com

Available online, *Primark Global Access* (former title: *Disclosure Global Access)* provides records of company annual reports through the SEC database, a fully searchable compilation of business and financial information for over 12,000 companies traded on major U.S. stock exchanges and Worldscope, providing information on companies headquartered in the U.S. and abroad. Also provides statistics for new issues, Canadian companies, brokerage house research reports, industry reports, company briefs, and U.S. private companies.

223. *Reuters.com* (http://www.reuters.com)

British-based site contains news releases, stock prices, and securities markets data. Their "Market Views" section include charts on performance and Risk Grade.

224. Standard & Poor's Corporation. *Analyst's Handbook.* New York: Standard & Poor's, 1964- Annual, with monthly supplements.

Provides approximately 20 financial statistics on a per share basis for various industry categories contained in the S & P 500. Designed to enable users to compare vital per share data and financial statistics for S & P Industrial Stocks with the 71 industries comprising the index.

225. Standard & Poor's Corporation. *Dividend Record.* New York: Standard & Poor's. daily with weekly, quarterly, and annual cumulations. Available in paper and microfiche formats and

online through *Standard & Poor's Net Advantage* (http://www.netadvantage.standardpoor.com)

Provides data on over 18,000 dividend paying issues, both common and preferred stock.

226. Standard & Poor's Corporation. *The Outlook.* New York: Standard & Poor's. Weekly.

Studies the outlook for financial and economic trends and for investment opportunities. Evaluates stocks for their investment potential and provides S & P Analysts' STARS rankings, including lists for rising stars, falling stars, and new stars. Provides statistical data for S & P monthly stock price indexes and market measures, among which are Nasdaq Composite and Dow Jones Industrials.

227. Standard & Poor's Corporation. *S & P 500 Directory.* New York: Standard & Poor's. Annual.

The S & P 500 is comprised of a representative sample of common stocks that trade on the NYSE, Amex, and OTC (including Nasdaq) markets. The 500 is a basket of a weighted average of stock prices and common shares outstanding. Explains calculation methodology and total return methodology. Provides an alphabetical listing of the 500 companies that comprise the S & P 500 Composite Price Index. For each company listed, the entry includes the ticker symbol, the S & P industry group, and a summary.

228. Standard & Poor's Corporation. *S & P 500 Information Bulletin.* New York: Standard & Poor's. Monthly.

Each issue includes a statistical summary of stock performance of the S & P 500 companies, including dividends, market value, shares, etc. Also presents news reports of events that have a bearing on the index, including mergers and acquisitions.

229. Standard & Poor's Corporation. *Stock Guide*. New York: Standard
     & Poor's, 1943- Monthly. Available in paper and microfiche
     formats, and online through *Standard & Poor's Net Advantage*
     (http://www.netadvantage.standardpoor.com)

Provides data for over 11,000 common and preferred stocks on
the New York Stock Exchange, the American Stock Exchange, Nasdaq,
etc. Data presented for: ticker symbol, name of company, where traded,
par value, S & P earnings and dividend records for common stocks,
financial position, price range, annual earnings, etc. Each issue features
economic and industrial profiles. Also provides statistics for over 750
mutual funds and 450 closed-end investment funds.

230. Standard & Poor's Corporation. *Stock Market Encyclopedia*. New
     York: Standard & Poor's. V. 1, 1962- Quarterly.

Features: S & P stock reports on approximately 750 of most
actively traded stocks; S & P Common Stock Ranking; a profile of the
S & P 500 Index; charts of the S & P Stock Indexes; articles on topics
of interest to investors; listings showing leading companies and
companies with highest yields; summary of companies' yearly stock
price ranges, etc.

231. Standard & Poor's Corporation. *Stock Reports NASDAQ and
     Regional Exchanges*. New York: Standard & Poor's, 1994-
     (Former title: *Standard & Poor's Stock Reports. Over the
     Counter*) available in paper format and online through Standard
     & Poor's Net Advantage.

Provides data for over 1500 of the most active companies traded
on Nasdaq and regional exchanges. Each record contains: overview,
stock price information, earnings per share data, income statement
analysis, balance sheet and other financial data, and company address
and phone number. Evaluates current company performance and
possible future developments.

232. Standard & Poor's Corporation. Trendline Daily Action Stock
Charts. New York: Standard & Poor's, 1959-   Weekly.

Covers 52 weeks of daily price-volume performance on over 720
stocks, including those traded on Nasdaq. Compares past performances
against the S & P 500 Index.

233. Statistical   Reference   Index   (SRI).   Bethesda,   Maryland:
Congressional Information Service, Inc., a member of the
LEXIS-NEXIS Family. V. 1- 1980- Monthly, with annual
cumulations. URL: http://www.cispubs.com Available online
through LEXIS-NEXIS's *Statistical Universe*

Issued in two parts, an Abstracts and an Index volume. Indexes
statistics from sources other than Federal Government Agencies.
Statistical sources are associations and institutes, business and
commercial publishers, state government agencies, research centers, and
universities. Indexes are by Subjects and Names, Category, Issuing
Source, and Publication Title. The accompanying Abstracts volume
provides bibliographic citations and addresses of publications as well
as a summary of the statistics source.

234. Stocks.com (http://www.stocks.com)

Some sections require registration. Extensive site links to Wall
Street analysts reports, real-time quotes, after hours trading statistics,
financial planning tools, company annual reports, business and market
news, etc.

235. StocksandNews.com (http://www.stocksandnews.com)

Contains articles about the previous week's developments in the
economy and in the stock markets; articles about immportant events in
Wall Street history; and an analysis of the business, economic, and
financial news by Dr. Allan F. Bortrum, Sci/Tech Editor of
StocksandNews.

236. *Streamer.* (http://www.streamer.com)

Provides real-time streaming quotes via Datek-powered quote engine. Requires registration.

237. *TheStreet.com* (http://www.thestreet.com)

Includes company news and market reports and provides analysis from TheStreet's A-team analysts.

238. *United & Babson Investment Report.* Wellesley Hills, Massachusetts: Babson-United Investment Advisors, Inc., 1919- Weekly.

Provides analysis of current economic and financial indicators; recommends stocks; projects trends in the markets; and profiles selected companies.

239. United States. Securities and Exchange Commission. *Edgar Database.* URL: http://www.sec.gov

Provides access to full-text reports of companies filed with the Securities and Exchange Commission. Includes 10K and 10Q reports. For most companies, coverage is currently 1994 to present. To gain access to the Edgar filles, first click on Search Edgar Archives, then Quick Forms Lookup.

240. *Value Line Investment Survey.* New York: Value Line, Inc. 1931- Weekly, available on microfiche, paper and electronic formats. URL: http:www.valueline.com

Investment advisory service registered with the Securities and Exchange Commission. Consists of three sections: Summary and Index, a weekly, alphabetical catalog of approximately 1700 stocks at their most recent prices and their current rankings for Timeliness and Safety; Selection and Opinion, which analyzes the outlook of the stock; and

Ratings and Reports which presents a full page report on each of the 1700 stocks. Data provided for each stock include: recent price; dividend yield; highest and lowest prices of the year; number of shares traded monthly; where traded; quarterly dividends paid; quarterly earnings; and capital structure. Statistics presented in the Selection and Opinion section include the Dow Jones Industrial Average; Gross National Product; and the Value Line Composite.

241. *Wall Street City* (http://www.wallstreetcity.com)

   Provides real-time quotes (requires registration), delayed-time quotes, major indexes, the day's hottest stocks, personal investment advice, stock charts, discussion boards, etc.

242. *Wall Street Journal.* New York: Dow Jones & Co., 1889- Daily (5/week) Available in print, microfilm, and electronic formats. URL: http://www.wsj.com

   In addition to articles and features about finance and investments, companies, and world news stories, provides market statistics in its "Money and Investing" section. The "Markets Diary" includes statistics on the Dow Jones Industrial Average, International Stocks, and the U.S. Dollar. Provides daily trading statistics for Nasdaq Small-Cap Issues and Nasdaq National Market Issues, plus the Nasdaq Composite Index. Features a year-end review of the markets. Online edition, *Wall Street Journal Interactive*, also available through subscription, provides the *Journal*, the *Journal's* Asian edition, *Barron's Online*, and allows searching of full-text database of Dow Jones.

243. *Wall Street Research Net* URL: http://www.wsrn.com

   Provides company news releases, market news, profile of company of the week, list of most active stocks, economic information, and portfolio tracking.

244. *Yahoo! Finance* (http://finance.yahoo.com)

Financial information site includes discussion board, delayed-time quotes, stock performance charts, and company data.

APPENDIX I
CHRONOLOGY OF
THE NASDAQ STOCK MARKET

1938 - Passage of the Maloney Act, which amended Section 15A of the Securities Exchange Act of 1934. Maloney Act calls for establishment of national securities associations that would serve as self-regulatory organizations (SROs).

1939 - National Association of Securities Dealers, Inc. (NASD) established.

1961 - Congress authorizes the U.S. Securities and Exchange Commission to conduct a special study of the securities markets.

1963 - Publication of the Special Study of Securities Markets of the Securities and Exchange Commission. Report recommends automation as a possible solution to fragmentation the SEC found in the OTC market. NASD is charged with implementation of automated system.

1966 - NASD forms an Automation Committee to study implementation of automated system.

1968 - NASD begins work on the National Association of Securities Dealers Automated Quotation (NASDAQ). Bunker-Ramo Corporation of Trumbull, Connecticut was selected to build and operate automated system, under NASD supervision.

1971 - On February 8, Nasdaq starts trading, with median quotes for 2500 OTC securities. Terminals of over 500 Market Makers nationwide are linked to central computer Trumbull, CT.

1976 - NASD acquires Nasdaq system from builder/operator Bunker Ramo Corporation.

1980 - In a major $22 million system upgrade, UNIVAC 1192s replace the UNIVAC 1122s, which doubles speed and trebling memory. Level II and III terminals are replaced with eight times display capacity and twice the speed, and made programmable.

1982 - Introduction of the National Market System (NMS), predecessor to the Nasdaq National Market.

1983 - Introduction of the Computer Assisted Execution System (CAES) and the Trade Acceptance and Reconciliation Service (TARS).

1984 - Implementation, on voluntary basis, of the Small Order Execution System (SOES), designed to provide automated execution of 500 shares or less.

1986 - Opening of the $17.3 million NASD Operations Center in Rockville, Maryland. The Center houses a full backup to the Trumbull, CT. Central Computer Complex.

1987 - Introduction of the Nasdaq Workstation, a PC-based platform, providing traders with greater flexibility and faster tool.

October 1987 market crash

1988 - Begins implementation on the Advanced Computer Execution System (ACES).

Participation in SOES made mandatory for all market makers in NMS issues.

Introduction of the Order Confirmation Transaction Service (OCT).

1989 - Introduction the Automated Conformation Transaction Service (ACT).

1990 - Introduction of the OTC Bulletin Board service by the NASD. The Bulletin Board provides access to securities and information about the securities, not listed on any national exchange.

1991 - Introduction of SelectNet, an online screen negotiation and execution service.

1992 - Implementation of Nasdaq International Service, an international extension of Nasdaq that operates during London and European trading hours.

1994 - Nasdaq surpasses the New York Stock Exchange in annual share volume.

Publication of academic research paper by William Christie and Paul Schultz, "Why do NASDAQ Market Makers Avoid Odd-Eighth Quotes?" *Journal of Finance*, December 1994. Results of research released to the press, May 1994. Study triggers investigations by Department of Justice and the SEC.

1995 - Release of Rudman Commission report, initiated by NASD and the SEC.

1996 - Establishment of NASD Regulation, Inc. (NASDR) in February as result of Rudman Commission recommendations.

Release of Federal investigation reports, triggered by Christie-Schultz study. Reports released by SEC and U.S. Department of Justice.

1997 - Implementation of new SEC Order Handling Rules.

1998 - Merger between NASD and the American Stock Exchange establishes the Nasdaq-Amex Market Group.

1999 - NASD Board of Governors approves restructuring of the NASD.

Opening of the Nasdaq Stock Market MarketSite facility in New York City.

2000 - Frank Zarb announces development of Super Montage for 2001.

Plans announced for decimalization of Nasdaq in 2001.

APPENDIX II
NASD/NASDAQ OFFICERS

Chairmen of the NASD Board of Governors:

1939 - B. Howell Griswold, Jr.
1940 - Francis A. Bonner
1941 - Robert W. Baird
1942 - H.H. Dewar
1943 - Henry G. Ritter III
1944 - Ralph Chapman Farwall
1945 - Ralph E. Phillips
1946 - William K. Barclay, Jr.
1947 - Herbert F. Boynton
1948 - L. Raymond Billett
1949 - Clement A. Evans
1950 - John J. Sullivan
1951 - Howard E. Behse
1952 - Clarence A. Bickel
1953 - Carl Stolle
1954 - Edward C. George
1955 - Harold E. Wood
1956 - Frank H. Hunter
1957 - Frank L. Reissner
1958 - Charles L. Bergmann
1959 - Alexander Yearley IV
1960 - Glenn E. Anderson
1961 - William H. Chaflin III

1962 - Avery Rockefeller, Jr.
1963 - Merrill M. Cohen
1963 - Hudson B. Lemkau
1964 - Robert W. Haack
1964 - Robert R. Miller
1965 - G. Shelby Friedrichs Howard
1966 - Allan C. Eustis, Jr.
1967 - Robert M. Gardiner
1968 - Phil E. Pearce
1969 - Kenneth H. Sayre
1970 - Gordon L. Teach
1971 - J. Coleman Budd
1972 - Peter C. Barnes
1973 - J. Logan Burke, Jr.
1974 - David R. Murphey III
1975 - Raymond A. Mason
1976 - Robert W. Swinarton
1977 - Eugene Arnold, Jr.
1978 - David W. Mesker
1979 - J. Stephen Putnam
1980 - James F. Keegan
1981 - L.C. Peterson Kirkpatrick
1982 - Ernest F. Rice, Jr.
1983 - Norman T. Wilde, Jr.
1984 - Carl P. Sherr
1985 - Peter D. Byrne
1986 - David W. Hunter
1987 - Joseph R. Hardiman
1987 - James M. Davin
1988 - Stephen L. Hammerman
1989 - William L. Tedford, Jr.
1990 - Kenneth J. Wessels
1991 - William B. Summers, Jr.
1992 - Charles B. Johnson
1993 - Fredric M. Roberts
1994 - Joseph J. Grano, Jr.
1995 - Ian B. Davidson
1996 - Mary Alice Brophy (Jan. - Apr.)
1996 - Daniel P. Tully (Apr.1996 - Apr. 1997)
1997 - Frank G. Zarb (Apr. 1997 to Present)

NASD Chief Executive Officers

1939-1964 - Wallace H. Fulton
1964-1967 - Robert W. Haack
1967-1970 - Robert B. Walbert
1970-1987 - Gordon S. Macklin
1987-1997 - Joseph R. Hardiman
1997-2000 - Frank G. Zarb
2000   - Robert R. Glauber (Nov. 2000 to Present)

NASDAQ Presidents and CEOs

1971-1986 - Gordon S. Macklin, President and CEO
1986-1996 - Joseph R. Hardiman, President and CEO
1996-2000 - Al Berkeley, President; Frank G. Zarb, CEO
2000 -   - Rick Ketchum. President; Hardwick Simmons, CEO

APPENDIX III
DIRECTORY OF OFFICE LOCATIONS
VISITORS CENTER

NASD/Nasdaq Offices

National Association of Securities Dealers, Inc. (NASD)
1735 K Street, N.W.
Washington, D.C.   20006-1500
Telephone: 202-728-8000
Inquiries: 301-590-6500
Fax No. : 202-293-6260

NASD/Nasdaq Financial Center
33 Whitehall Street
New York, N.Y.   10004-2193
Telephone: 212-858-4000
Fax No. : 212-509-8436

NASD/NASD Regulation, Inc.
1390 Piccard Drive
Rockville, MD   20850
Telephone: 301-590-6500

NASD/NASD Regulation, Inc.
5 Choke Cherry Road
Rockville, MD 20850
Telephone: 301-417-6540

NASD Operations Center
9513 Key West Avenue
Rockville, MD 20850
Telephone: 301-590-6500
Fax No. : 301-590-6705

NASD/The Nasdaq Stock Market, Inc.
15201 Diamondback Drive
Rockville, MD 20850
Telephone: 301-590-6500

NASD/The Nasdaq Stock Market, Inc.
9801 Washingtonian Blvd.
Gaithersburg, MD 20878
Telephone: 301-590-6500

The Nasdaq Stock Market, Inc.
1735 K Street, N.W.
Washington, D.C. 20006-1500
Telephone: 202-496-2500
Fax No.   202-496-2696

The Nasdaq Stock Market, Inc.
33 Whitehall Street
New York, N.Y. 10004-2193
Telephone: 212-858-4000
Fax No.   212-858-3980

The Nasdaq Stock Market, Inc.
2500 Sandhill Road, Suite 220
Menlo Park, CA   94025
Telephone: 415-233-2000
Fax No. : 415-233-2099

Nasdaq International, Ltd.
Durrant House
8/13 Chiswell Street
London ECIY 4UQ
United Kingdom
Telephone: 44 (171) 374-6969
Fax No. : 44 (171)374-4488

Nasdaq Media Relations
1735 K Street, N.W.
Washington, D.C.   20006-1500
Telephone: 202-728-8884
Fax No.:   202-728-6993

Nasdaq Technology Center
80 Merritt Boulevard
Trumbull, CT   06611
Telephone: 203-385-6502

Visitors' Center

Nasdaq MarketSite
43rd Street and Broadway
New York, N.Y.
Telephone: 877-627-3271

Presents MarketSite, a high-tech interactive experience to introduce
visitors to future of investing. Open seven days a week, allows visitors
to play an interactive investing game, view stock quotes, visit NASD

and Nasdaq web sites, view live news broadcasts by CNNfn, MSNBC, CNBC, and others during market hours. Features gift shop to purchase tee shirts, pens, etc.

NASD Regulation District Offices

District 1

525 Market Street, Suite 300
San Francisco, CA   94105-2711
Telephone: 415-882-1200
Fax No. : 415-546-6991

District 2

300 S. Grand Ave., Suite 1600
Los Angeles, CA   90071
Telephone: 213-627-2122
Fax No. : 213-617-3299

District 3

Republic Office Building
370 17th Street, Suite 2900
Denver, CO 80202-5629
Telephone: 303-446-3100
Fax No. : 303-620-9450

Two Union Square
601 Union Street, Suite 1616
Seattle, WA 98101-2327
Telephone: 206-624-0790
Fax No. : 206-623-2518

District 4

12 Wyandotte Plaza
120 West 12th Street, Suite 900
Kansas City, MO 64105
Telephone: 816-421-5700
Fax No.: 816-421-5029

District 5

1100 Poydras Street
Suite 850, Energy Centre
New Orleans, LA 70163
Telephone: 504-522-6527
Fax No. : 504-522-4077

District 6

12801 North Central Expwy.
Suite 1050
Dallas, TX 75243
Telephone: 972-701-8554
Fax No.: 972-716-7646

District 7

One Securities Centre
3490 Piedmond Road, N.E.
Suite 500
Atlanta, GA 30305
Telephone: 404-239-6100
Fax No. : 404-237-9290

District 8

10 S. LaSalle St., 20th Floor
Chicago, IL   60603-1002
Telephone: 312-899-4400
Fax No. : 312-236-3025

Renaissance on Playhouse Sq .
1350 Euclid Avenue
Suite 650
Cleveland, OH   44115
Telephone: 216-694-4545
Fax No. : 216-694-3048

District 9

11 Penn Center
1835 Market Street, 19th Floor
Philadelphia, PA   19103
Telephone: 215-665-1180
Fax No. : 215-496-0434

581 Main Street, 7th Floor
Woodbridge, NJ 07095
Telephone: 732-596-2000
Fax No. : 732-596-2001

District 10

33 Whitehall Street
New York, NY 10004-2193
Telephone: 212-858-4000
Fax No. : 212-858-4189

District 11

260 Franklin Street, 16th Floor
Boston, MA   02110
Telephone: 617-261-0800
Fax No. : 617-951-2337

APPENDIX IV
THE NASD/NASDAQ FAMILY OF WEB SITES

NASD (http://www.nasd.com)

The parent site. Provides current news reports, historical information about NASD and Nasdaq, academic research papers (most in full text) from both NASD and other affiliations, glossary of terms, list of publications for sale, full text of the most recent annual report, securities industry regulatory information, and biographies of key officers. Provides links to NASD's "online community of resources," and an annotated listing of links to Nasdaq, AMEX, OTC markets, etc.

NASD Academic Research (http://www.academic.nasd.com)

Links to NASD working papers and an academic forum, featuring selected articles and papers. Selected documents are available in full-text format.

NASD Career Opportunities (http://www.careers.nasd.com)

Search by company, location, and job title to find job opportunities. Includes information about benefits, compensation, and equal employment opportunity policy. Provides addresses for mailing resumes.

NASD Dispute Resolution (http://www.nasdadr.com)

Site representing the largest securities dispute resolution forum in the United States. Contains press releases, advice on how to start a mediation/arbitration, rules and procedures of NASD's arbitration and mediation programs, career opportunities, recent arbitration and mediation statistics of NASD, FAQs, and the Code of Arbitration Procedure.

NASD Regulation (http://www.nasdr.com)

"A Resource for Investors and the Securities Industry." Official site of NASD Regulation, Inc., an independent subsidiary of NASD, Inc. Provides names and addresses of district offices and contacts, press releases, career opportunities, securities industry links, glossary of terms, enforcement actions, rule filings index, margin statistics, and the public disclosure program, designed to assist investors in their selection of a broker or securities firm.

Nasdaq Euromarket (http://www.nasdaq-euromarket.com)

A joint market, provides trading statistics for both Nasdaq and European stock exchanges.

Nasdaq InterMarket (http://www.intermarket.nasdaqtrader.com)

The Nasdaq Intermarket, formerly known as the Third Market, is comprised of multiple Nasdaq market participants that quote and trade securities listed on the NYSE and Amex using their proprietary systems, Nasdaq technology, and the InterMarket Trading System (ITS). Their web site provides current news reports, how to subscribe to the Nasdaq InterMarket, statistics, full text user guides, etc.

Nasdaq-Japan (http://www.nasdaq-japan.com)

Provides market statistics for Japanese exchanges and for Nasdaq. Text in English and Japanese.

Nasdaq Newsroom (http://www.nasdaq-amexnews.com

Contains full-text of key reports including most recent NASD annual report, major speeches, links to selected academic studies, market statistics, and press releases. Available in English, German, French, and Spanish. Includes one section open to registered news reporters only.

Nasdaq Trader (http://www.nasdaqtrader.com)

"The premier site for Nasdaq trading information" contains history and news about trading halts, trader news--current headlines, first day trading information for new public companies, extended hours trading statistics, fee-based historical reports of statistics, searchable ticker symbol directory, glossary of terms, FAQs, e-mail and phone number for help desk. Includes some fee-based components.

Nasdaq Stock Market, Inc. (http://www.nasdaq.com)

Provides statistics including most active stocks; major indices; Dow Jones Industrial Average; statistical charts and tables for intraday and comparison charts for 3, 6, and 12 months; stock quotes for Nasdaq, Amex, NYSE, and Over-the-Counter Bulletin Board (OTCBB). Also includes recent IPOs; investor tools, which provide tracking of private portfolios and investments; news reports; glossary; global markets data; and company news. The "About Nasdaq" section features access to its mission statement, historical timeline, order handling rules, benefits of listing on Nasdaq, and how a trade is executed. Available in full-text format are: "Nasdaq in Black and White," an illustrated guide to procedures and organization; recent NASD annual reports; NASD Sanction Guidelines, selected speeches, and press releases.

Nasdaq United Kingdom (http://www.nasdaq-amex.co.uk)

Contains statistics for Nasdaq and United Kingdom stock exchanges. Includes press releases.

APPENDIX V
DIRECTORY OF
SERIAL PUBLICATIONS

The following are selected serial publications with information about Nasdaq, with names of publishers, addresses, frequency, and selected business titles where publication is indexed. Because of the often rapidly changing prices of the publications, annual subscription costs and/or costs per issue have not been included. Articles from some of the titles listed here are included as annotated entries; other titles have been presented in the chapter covering statistical sources. This is a selected list of serial publications; additional titles can be located by scanning indexes, abstracts, and databases.

The Banker
Financial Times Business Information
2 Greystoke Pl.
Fetter Ln.
London EC4A IND
United Kingdom
V. 1, 1926- Monthly
Indexed in: *Business Periodicals Index, Business Index, Trade and Industry Index, Key to Economic Science, World Bank Abstracts.* Also available online through Bell and Howell Information and Learning

Barron's: the Dow Jones Business and Financial Weekly
Dow Jones & Co., Inc.
200 Liberty Street
New York, N.Y.   10281
URL: http://www.barrons.com
V. 1, 1921- Weekly
Indexed in:*Business Periodicasl Index, Business Index, Magazine IndexTrade and Industry Index.* Also available online through Dow JonesNews.

Better Investing
National Association of Investors Corp.
P.O. Box 220
Royal Oak, Michigan   48067
URL: http://www.better-investing.org
V. 1, 1951-

Bloomberg Personal Finance
Bloomberg Financial Markets
100 Business Park Drive
Box 888
Princeton, N.J.   08542
URL: http://www.bloomberg.com
V. 1, 1996- Monthly
Archived   articles   available   to   subscribers,   online   at:
http://www.bloomberg.com/personal/archive.html

The Boston Globe
New York Times Co./Globe Newspaper Co.
135 Morrissey Boulevard
P.O. Box 2378
Boston, Massachusetts   02107
URL: http://www.boston.com/globe
V. 1, 1872-   Daily
Also available online through Dialog, DataTimes, COMPUSERV, LEXIS-NEXIS.

Business Week
McGraw-Hill Companies
1221 Avenue of the Americas
39th Floor
New York, N.Y. 10020
V. 1, 1929- Weekly
Indexed in: *ABI/INFORM, Academic Index, Accounting and Tax Index, Banking Literature Index, Book Review Index, Business Periodicals Index, Business Index, Future Survey, Key to Economic Science, Management Contents, Microcomputer Abstracts, PAIS, Reader's Guide to Periodical Literature, Trade and Industry Index, Work Related Abstracts.* Also available online through vendors Dialog Corporation, Dow Jones News Interactive, Lexis-Nexis, NewsNet, Uncover.

The Economist
Economist Newspaper Ltd.
25 St. James's Street
London, SW1 1HA
United Kingdom
URL: http://www.economist.com
V. 1, 1843- Weekly - 51/yr.
Indexed in: *Business Periodicals Index, ABI/INFORM, Book Review Digest, Anbar, PROMT.* Also available online through Bell and Howell Information and Learning, Gale Group, Media Stream, Inc.

Equities
Equities Magazine, Inc.
160 Madison Avenue
3rd Floor
New York, N.Y. 10016
V. 1, 1951- Monthly
URL: http://www.equities.com
Indexed in: *PROMT*

Financial Analysts Journal
Association for Investment Management and Research
Box 3668
Charlottesville, Virginia   22903
V. 1, 1945- Bi-Monthly
Indexed in:*Accounting and Tax Index, Business Periodicals Index, Business Index, Computer Literature Index, Management Contents.* Also available online through Bell & Howell.

Financial Times (North American edition)
The Financial Times, Inc.
1330 Avenue of the Americas
New York, N.Y.   10019
URL: http://www.ft.com
V. 1, 1985-   Daily (Monday-Saturday)
Indexed in: *Management and Marketing Abstracts.* Also available on CD-ROM through Chadwyck Healey Corporation.

Forbes
Forbes, Inc.
60 Fifth Avenue
New York, N.Y.   10011
URL: http://www.forbes.com/forbes
V. 1, 1917- Bi-Weekly
Indexed in: *ABI/INFORM, Academic Index, Accounting and Tax Index, Business Index, Business Periodicals Index, Key to Economic Science,* Management Contents. Also available online through Dialog Corporation, Dow Jones Interactive, Gale Group, Bell and Howell.

Fortune
Time, Inc.
Business Information Group
1271 Avenue of the Americas
New York, N.Y.   10020
URL: http://www.fortune.com
V. 1, 1930-   Bi-Weekly
Indexed in: *ABI/INFORM, Business Index, Business Periodicals Index,*

*Accounting and Tax Index, PAIS, Trade and Industry
Index.* Also available online through LEXIS-NEXIS, H.W. Wilson,
Bell and Howell Information and Learning.

The Handbook of Nasdaq Stocks
Mergent FIS
60 Madison Avenue
6th Floor
New York, N.Y.   10010
V. 1, 1999- Quarterly

Institutional Investor
Euromoney Publications plc
4-5 Deans Ct.
London ECRV SHX
England
URL: http://www.euromoney.com
V. 1, 1967- Monthly
Indexed in: *ABI/INFORM, Business Index, Key to Economic Science,
Management Contents, PAIS, Risk Abstracts, Trade and Industry Index,
World Bank Abstracts.* Also available online through Information
Access Co.

Investment Dealers' Digest
Securities Data Publishing, Inc.
40 W. 57th Street
11th Floor
New York, N.Y.   10019
V. 1, 1935-   Weekly
Indexed in: *PAIS, PROMT.* Also available online through Information
Access Co. and Bell & Howell.

Investor Relations Business Newsletter
Securities Data Publishing
40 W. 57th Street
11th Floor

New York, N.Y.   10019
V. 1, 1996- Bi-Weekly

Investors' Digest
Institute for Econometric Research
2200 W. 10th Street
Deerfield Beach, Florida   33442
V. 1, 1989- Monthly

Journal of Finance
Blackwell Publishers
350 Main Street
Malden, Massachusetts   02148
V. 1, 1946- Bi-Monthly
Indexed in: *ABI/INFORM, Accounting and Tax Index, Business Periodicals Index, Business Index, Journal of Economic Literature, Key to Economic Science, Management and Marketing Abstracts, Management Contents, PAIS., Risk Abstracts, Trade and Industry Index, World Bank Abstracts.* Also available online through JSTOR, UnCover, Bell & Howell Information and Learning, Genuine Article, SWETS.

Journal of Financial and Quantitative Economics
University of Washington
School of Business Administration
15 Lewis Hall
Box 353200
Seattle, Washington   98195
V. 1, 1966- 4/yr.
Indexed in:*ABI/INFORM, Accounting and Tax Index, Anbar, Business Periodicals Index, Library Literature, Management Contents, Risk Abstracts, Trade and Industry Index.* Also available online through Genuine Article, SWETS, Bell & Howell Information and Learning, UnCover

Journal of Financial Economics
Elsevier Science SA
P.O. Box 564
Lausannc, 1001
Switzerland
V. 1, 1974- Monthly
Indexed in: *ABI/INFORM, Anbar, Business Index, Journal of Economic Literature, Management Contents, Risk Abstracts, Trade and Industry Index, World Bank Abstracts.* Also available online through Science Direct.

Journal of Financial Research
Virginia Polytechnic Institute and State University
College of Business
Department of Finance
1016 Pamplin Hall
Blacksburg, Virginia   24061
URL: http://www.vt.edu
V. 1, 1978- Quarterly
Indexed in: *ABI/INFORM, Anbar, Business Periodicals Index, Journal of Economic Literature, Risk Abstracts.* Also available online through Information Access Co., Genuine Article, SWETS, Bell & Howell Information and Learning, UnCover.

Journal of Investing
Institutional Investor
488 Madison Avenue
New York, N.Y.   10022
V. 1, 1992-
Indexed in: *Business Periodicals Index, ABI/INFORM.* Also available online through Bell and Howell Information and Learning, H.W.Wilson

Journal of Portfolio Management
Institutional Investor
488 Madison Avenue
New York, N.Y.   10022
V. 1, 1975- Quarterly

Indexed in: *ABI/INFORM, Business Index, Anbar, Management Contents, Journal of Economic Literature.* Also available online through Bell and Howell Information and Learning, H.W. Wilson, Gale Group

Kiplingers Personal Finance
Kiplinger Washington Editors, Inc.
1729 H Street, N.W.
Washington, D.C.   20006
URL: http://www.kiplinger.com
V. 1, 1947- Monthly
Former title (until 1991): *Changing Times*
Indexed in: *PAIS, Business Periodicals Index, Magazine Index*
Also available online through Bell and Howell Information and Learning, Dialog Corporation, Gale Group, LEXIS-NEXIS, Northern Light Technology, Inc., H.W. Wilson

The Los Angeles Times
Times Mirror Square
Los Angeles, California   90053
URL: http://www.latimes.com
V. 1, 1881-   Daily
Also available online through Dialog, LEXIS-NEXIS

Louis Rukeyser's Wall Street
Louis Rukeyser's Wall Street Club
1750 Old Meadow Rd.
Ste. 300
McLean, Virginia   22102
http://www.rukeyser.com
V. 1, 1962-   Monthly

Money
Time, Inc.
Time & Life Building
Rockefeller Center
New York, N.Y.   10020

URL: http://www.money.com
V. 1, 1972- Monthly
Indexed in: *Business Periodicals Index, PAIS, Readers Guide to Periodical Literature, Banking Literature Index, Trade and Industry Index.*

Nasdaq Subscriber Bulletin
National Association of Securities Dealers, Inc.
1735 K Street, N.W.
Washington, D.C.   20006
Quarterly newsletter

The New York Times
The New York Times Co.
229 W. 43rd Street
New York, N.Y.   10036
URL: http://www.nytimes.com
V. 1, 1851- Daily
Also available online through Bell & Howell Information and Learning, Dow Jones News Retrieval

The Online Investor
Online Investor
1515 W. 22nd Street
Suite 475
Oak Brook, Illinois   60523
URL: http://www.onlineinvestor.com
Monthly, except January/February; July/August

The Outlook
Standard & Poor's Corporation
25 Broadway
New York, N.Y.   10004
V. 1, 1937- Weekly.

Pensions and Investments
Crain Communications, Inc.
220 East 42nd Street
New York, N.Y.   10017
V. 1, 1973- Fortnightly
Indexed in: *ABI/INFORM, Business Periodicals Index, PROMT, Trade and Industry Index*; Also available online through Information Access Co., LEXIS-NEXIS

Review of Financial Economics
Elsevier Science Ltd.
The Boulevard
Langford Ln.
Kidlington, Oxon
OX5 1GB
United Kingdom
V. 1, 1965- Three times per year
Former title (until 1991): *Review of Business and Economics Research*
Indexed in: *Journal of Economic Literature, PAIS, ABI/INFORM, Accounting and Tax Index, Business Index, Management Contents, Risk Abstracts*

Review of Securities and Commodities Regulation
Standard & Poor's Corporation
55 Water Street
New York, N.Y.   10041
V. 1, 1967- Semi-Monthly/22 issues per year
Former title (until 1985): *Standard & Poor's Review of Securities Regulation*

SEC News Digest
U.S. Securities and Exchange Commission
450 Fifth Street, N.W.
MISC-11
Washington, D.C.   20549
Distributed by:
Washington Service Bureau

1225 Connecticut Avenue, N.W.
Washington, D.C.   20036
URL: http://www.sec.gov/ndighome.htm
Daily
Also available online through SEC, Bureau of National Affairs

Securities Regulation Law Journal
West Group
629 Opperman Drive
Eagan, Minnesota 55123
V. 1, 1973- Quarterly
URL: http://www.westgroup.com
Indexed in: *ABI/INFORM, Business Index, Accounting and Tax Index, Management Contents, Trade and Industry Index*

Securities Week
McGraw-Hill Companies
1221 Avenue of the Americas
New York, N.Y. 10020
V. 1, 1973- Weekly
Also available online through Dow Jones Interactive, Dialog Corporation, LEXIS-NEXIS, Northern Light Technology, Inc.

Standard & Poor's Analyst's Handbook
Standard & Poor's Corporation
55 Water Street
New York, N.Y. 10041
V. 1, 1964-   Annual, with monthly updates

Standard & Poor's Daily Stock Price Record. Nasdaq
Standard & Poor's Corporation
55 Water Street
New York, N.Y. 10041
V. 1, 1968- Quarterly
Former title: *Daily Stock Price Record. Over-the-Counter*
Available in print and microfiche formats.

Standard & Poor's Stock Guide
Standard & Poor's Corporation
55 Water Street
New York, N.Y. 10041
V. 1, 1943- Monthly
Former title: *Standard & Poor's Security Owner's Stock Guide*

Standard & Poor's Stock Reports. Nasdaq and Regional Exchanges
Standard & Poor's Corporation
55 Water Street
New York, N.Y.   10041
V. 1, 1934- Approx 4/yr.
Former title: *Standard & Poor's Stock Reports. Over the Counter*
Also available online through Standard & Poor's NetAdvantage
(http://www.netadvantage.standardpoor.com)

Stock Market Encyclopedia
Standard & Poor's Corporation
55 Water Street
New York, N.Y.   10041
V. 1, 1962- Quarterly
Former title (until 1985): *S & P Stock Market Encyclopedia*

Ticker
Investment Investor Group, Inc.
125 Broad Street
14th Floor
New York, N.Y.   10019
V. 1, 1996-   Monthly

Trendline Daily Action Stock Charts
Standard & Poor's Corporation
55 Water Street
New York, N.Y.   10041
V. 1, 1959-

United & Babson Investment Report
Babson-United Investment Advisors, Inc.
101 Prescott Street
Wellesley Hills, Massachusetts   02181
URL: http://www.babson.com
V. 1, 1919-   Weekly
Indexed in: *PROMT*

Value Line Investment Survey
Value Line Publishing, Inc.
220 East 42nd Street
New York, N.Y.   10017
URL: http://www.valueline.com
V. 1, 1931 Weekly
Available in print, online, microfiche, and CD-ROM.

Wall Street and Technology
Miller Freedman Inc.
One Penn Plaza
New York, N.Y.   10019
V. 1, 1983-   Monthly
Former title (until 1992): *Wall Street Computer Review*
Also available online through Bell and Howell Information and
Learning, Gale Group

Wall Street Journal
Dow Jones & Co., Inc.
200 Liberty Street
New York, N.Y.   10007
V. 1, 1889-   Daily (5/week)
URL: http://www.wsj.com
Indexed in: *PAIS, Book Review Index, Banking Literature
Index*. Also available online through Dow Jones/News Retrieval and
through Wall Street Journal's web site, *Wall Street Journal Interactive*.

Wall Street Letter
Institutional Investor Newsletters
477 Madison Avenue
New York, N.Y.   10022
V. 1, 1969- Weekly

Wall Street Transcript
Wall Street Transcript Corp.
100 Wall Street
New York, N.Y.   10005
V. 1, 1963- Weekly
URL: http://www.twst.com
Indexed in: *PROMT, Trade and Industry Index*

APPENDIX VI
INDEXES, ABSTRACTS, AND
FULL-TEXT DATABASES

The following is a selection of indexes, abstracts, and full-text databases. These specifically are for accessing articles in periodicals and newspapers. Statistical databases are listed and described in Chapter VIII.

ABI/INFORM Global. Source: Bell & Howell. Indexes and abstracts approximately business and management journals. Provides full-text coverage for approximately 600 journals. Available through Bell & Howell Proquest Direct, Dialog Corporation, Data-Star, LEXIS-NEXIS.

Business Index. Source: Information Access Company, a subsidiary of Thomson Corporation. Available on CD-ROM and online through Dialog Corporation, LEXIS-NEXIS. Indexes over 800 business, trade, and management journals, including *Wall Street Journal.*

Business Newsstand Source. Source: Dow Jones. Online database covers the day's global and financial news from newspapers, business magazines and includes *Wall Street Journal, Washington Post, Los Angeles Times,* and Economist.

Business Periodicals Index. Source: H.W. Wilson, Co. Available in print, CD-ROM, and online formats. Covers fields of accounting, finance and economics, banking, management, marketing, etc. Carried by vendors: Dialog Corp., OCLC, Wilsonline, and Silver Platter.

Business Source Premier. Source: EBSCOhost. Contains indexing, abstracting and some full-text coverage for business journals. Contains full-text for approximately 1650 journals. Also provides coverage of wire sources.

Dialog@Carl. Source: Dialog@Carl. Provides some full-text coverages of business journals and newspapers. Titles covered include *Los Angeles Times, American Banker Financial Publications, and AP News.*

JSTOR. Source: JSTOR. Provides full-text coverage of scholarly journals in economics and finance among which are: *Journal of Finance, Journal of Business, Review of Financial Studies,* and *Journal of Money, Credit, and Banking.*

Journal of Economic Literature. Source: American Economic Association. Indexes scholarly journals covering economics and finance. Available in print, CD-ROM and online formats. ECONLIT provides coverage of journal citations from *Journal of Economic Literature* plus books, dissertations, and collective volume citations.

LEXIS-NEXIS Academic Universe. Source: LEXIS-NEXIS, a division of Reed Elsevier, Inc. Includes section on Business, which contains full-text coverage of articles from newspapers and journals; full-text coverage of accounting journals and literature; SEC filings; news of over 25 industries; trade show information; and company data. Its section on Legal Research provides full-text coverage of law reviews; securities regulation and legal aspects of securities are covered in the law reviews.

PROMT (Predicasts Overview of Markets and Technology). Source: Gale Group. Contains abstracts and full-text records from trade and business journals, newspapers, business and industry newsletters, market research studies, investment analysts' reports, and Japanese news service.

Predicasts F & S Index United States. Source: Information Access Company, a division of Thomson Corporation. Available in print, CD-ROM, and online formats. Provides an index to product, company, industry, and market publications reported in business publications. Available online through Dialog, Data-Star.

ScienceDirect. Source: Elsevier. Provides full-text coverage of scholarly journals in economics and finance journals. Titles covered include: *Journal of Financial Economics, Journal of Financial Markets, Review of Financial Economics,* and *Quarterly Review of Economics and Finance.*

The Wall Street Journal Index. Issued with *Barron's Index.* Source: Bell & Howell. Annual, plus monthly updates. Abstracts and indexes articles and columns from *Wall Street Journal* and *Barron's.* Available in paper, CD-ROM, and online formats.

AUTHOR INDEX

Numbers refer to entry numbers, not to page numbers

TITLE INDEX

Numbers refer to entry numbers, not to page numbers

SUBJECT INDEX
Numbers refer to entry numbers, not to page numbers